PRAISE FOR *THERE IS NO GOD AND MARY IS HIS MOTHER*

"Warning! Handle this timely exploration of 'religionless Christianity' with care. Its potent medicine provides a wise and witty—yet deadly serious—antidote to mindless dogmatism, heartless moralism, and other forms of toxic religiosity. Follow the recommended daily dose of living in, with, and for Mystery, and be well on your way to spiritual recovery and relief."

—Marvin Ellison, author of *Making Love Just:*
Sexual Ethics for Perplexing Times

"Cathcart has written just the kind of book I have been trying to write for many years, but have only rarely succeeded. He has an impressive ability to convey demanding theological ideas in an accessible idiom without watering down the substance. I appreciate his skill in weaving in his own experiences, giving the book a personal voice and making his ideas more available.

Since I am a disciple (in a way) of both my predecessor at Harvard, George Santayana, and of Dietrich Bonhoeffer, and since I believe both have something vital to say to us today, I was worried at first to see how Cathcart draws on them. But he does it with verve and acuity, and here and there with genuine humor. He understands them both. But he also knows what is happening in the postmodern soul, somewhere between faith and skepticism. This honest and spirited book will speak to a varied lot of readers. I know that I will recommend it."

—Harvey Cox, Hollis Professor of Divinity, emeritus,
Harvard University, and author of *The Secular City*,
The Future of Faith, and *The Market as God*

"In a world swirling in supremacy culture, we don't need more religion; we need an ethics of engagement. This book helps us navigate how to embody an ethics of engagement from a place of care of self and other. A religionless world will be an okay world—if we embody an ethics of engagement."

—Robyn Henderson-Espinoza, PhD, founder and activist, Theology Project; author of *Activist Theology*; transqueer actixist; Latinx scholar; and public theologian

THERE IS **NO GOD**
AND MARY IS HIS MOTHER

THERE IS NO GOD AND MARY IS HIS MOTHER

REDISCOVERING RELIGIONLESS CHRISTIANITY

THOMAS CATHCART

FORTRESS PRESS
MINNEAPOLIS

THERE IS NO GOD AND MARY IS HIS MOTHER
Rediscovering Religionless Christianity

Unless otherwise noted, scripture quotations are from the New
Revised Standard Version of the Bible, copyright © 1989 National
Council of the Churches of Christ in the United States of
America. Used by permission. All rights reserved worldwide.

Scripture quotations marked (KJV) are from the King James
Version.

Cover image: sedmak/iStock
Cover design: Brice Hemmer

Print ISBN: 978-1-5064-7416-8
eBook ISBN: 978-1-5064-7417-5

TO MY FAVORITE ATHEIST,

DANNY KLEIN:

oldest and dearest friend for over sixty years,
collaborator on several books,
mentor on this one,
raised a secular Jew,
but a man to whom I often say,
"You're a better Christian than I am, my friend."

CONTENTS

CONTENTS

ACKNOWLEDGMENTS

I want to reiterate my gratitude to Danny Klein, dearest friend since 1957, for his constant guidance in the writing of this book. His unflagging encouragement and his close reading of several drafts were both crucial to its completion. The fact that he is himself the author of dozens of books didn't hurt.

Heartfelt thanks as well to my wife, Eloise, an excellent writer and editor in her own right, for her clear-eyed critique of an early draft and for her unfailing love for the last twenty-five years. Both Eloise and Danny come out of religious traditions different from mine, and their perspectives were invaluable.

Thank you to my wonderful daughter, Esther, for her permission to use a very personal story. Living within a short drive of each other, as we now do, has been a huge gift.

Bob Lohbauer, actor extraordinaire, thank you as well for the use of a poignant, personal anecdote.

Julia Lord, you have been Danny's and my talented (and sometimes relentless) agent for the past fifteen years. Even more importantly, you've been a dear friend. Thank you.

Many editors are good at improving their authors' prose style, and Ryan Hemmer at Fortress is one of the best of them. Never have I had an editor, though, who also knows the subject matter better than I do! That has been a huge boon, and I thank you, Ryan. Needless to mention, any remaining errors are mine.

INTRODUCTION

We are moving toward a completely religionless time; people as they are now simply cannot be religious anymore. . . . If religion is only a garment of Christianity—and even this garment has looked very different at different times—then what is a religionless Christianity?

—Dietrich Bonhoeffer, *Letters and Papers from Prison*

It's no secret that a growing number of people have stopped believing in the God they learned about in Sunday school. A recent study by a political scientist at Eastern Illinois University found that 23 percent of Americans now claim no religion, putting this group (the so-called Nones) in a three-way tie for first place with those who identify as Catholic or evangelical. Meanwhile, the mainline Protestant population—once the plurality of Americans—has fallen from 28 percent to 11 percent.

It's a puzzling time, not only for some "Nones," but also for some related groups: the Nearly Nones, the

Sometime Nones, the Borderline Nones—those with one religious foot inside the church and one skeptical foot outside. Their puzzlement, in turn, makes it a challenging time for church leaders, teachers, clergy, and college and seminary instructors, who, in addition to the obvious leadership challenges, are often wrestling with their own skepticism, questioning both their personal commitment to the faith and their vocation.

As a one-time teacher, sometime church leader, sometime dropout, and current church member, my journey may be of interest. Although I am not a "None," my story does intersect in many ways with those in the "no religion" group. I grew up in the mainline Protestant tradition, was active in Sunday school, was president of my youth group, and was accepting of what might be called the suburban-American-Protestant standard model of beliefs and practice in the 1950s. My plan was to become a Christian minister, the pastor of a church.

Like countless other adolescents, I found my faith challenged in college. In my freshman year at Harvard, I took a course called Ideas of Man and the World in Western Thought, in which we read the Greek tragedies, the Bible, and some Shakespeare, but mainly we read some of the highlights from the history of Western philosophy: samples from the works of Plato, Augustine, Descartes, Hume, Kant, Sartre, and others.

It was David Hume's *Dialogues concerning Natural Religion* that sent me into a tailspin. There, Hume systematically destroys all the traditional arguments for the existence of God. The one that I found most devastating was his attack on the "argument from design." That argument goes roughly like this: the intricacy of the universe is analogous to the intricacy of objects of human invention, which would therefore lead us to assume an analogous designer. This is the core of the current argument for "intelligent design" that leads some evangelical Christians to argue that our public schools should teach intelligent design alongside the theory of evolution.

Hume levels several objections. How can anything be said to be analogous to a one-off entity like the universe? Aren't there equally compelling analogies (e.g., the universe resembles an animal at least as closely as it does an object of human design) that would lead us to different conclusions about its origin? Even if we established the existence of a human-like designer "god," what would make one think that this designer is the traditional Judeo-Christian God, the God of Abraham, Isaac, and Jacob?

My head swam. I was fascinated by philosophy and went on to major in it.

Insofar as I had thought about it at all, I guess I had more or less relied on the argument from design to underlie my faith. One would think that, scrambled as my head was by Hume, I would have rethought my plan to go to divinity school. But I didn't. Probably because one evening I sat up all night and read Paul Tillich's *The Courage to Be* from start to finish. Tillich describes faith as something more like concern and courage than "belief in unbelievable statements." Along with my Jewish/atheist BFF, Danny Klein, I signed up for Tillich's course on the philosophies and religions of the Hellenistic period. (Danny's scientist father exclaimed, "I'm paying all this money for you to take a theology course!" Harvard tuition at the time was $1,250 a year.) The next year I went on to the University of Chicago Divinity School, where, shortly afterward, Tillich came to fill out the remainder of his career. (I like to say Tillich "followed me" to the University of Chicago.) Needless to say, I took every course of his I could.

(At the end of my second year, I dropped out after it became clear that I was not being called to pastoral ministry.)

The Truth of Atheism

Here is the situation as I now see it. Most critiques of faith by people outside the church (and those of us on the borderline) seem to be reactions to the *mythology* of Christianity, the system of *beliefs* eventually codified into *doctrines* and, in some cases, into *dogma*. This mythology supposedly defines what Christians should—or, at the dogma end of the scale, must— believe in order to call themselves Christians. Many atheists, as well as some interesting new associations of disillusioned, dropout ministers, start from the premise that in the twenty-first century, these beliefs are simply no longer believable. I agree. My only point of dissent (at least on a good day) is that I don't think these beliefs represent the essence of Christianity.

In the latter part of the twentieth century, the so-called New Atheists attacked these beliefs as basically irrational, nonscientific holdovers from a prescientific age. Among these beliefs are

- creation of the world by a supernatural being;
- a supposedly omnipotent and loving God, who apparently tolerates undeserved misery;
- miracles, particularly so-called nature miracles;
- the notion that this supernatural being had a preexisting son;
- the virgin birth;
- the resurrection of Jesus of Nazareth;
- the resurrection of all or some of the rest of us;
- the sacrificial death of Jesus of Nazareth as atonement—payment—for our sins;

- the second coming of Christ;
- the church as an institution "called out of" the world;
- the subordination of women;
- prejudice against gay, lesbian, and gender-nonconforming persons;
- the efficacy of intercessory prayer; and
- the belief that Christianity is the "one true religion."

Many of these are among the beliefs that no longer resonate with members of the Clergy Project, an online forum and support group for religious professionals who have discovered they are no longer able to believe in God. The Clergy Project was founded by people like John Compere, a fifth-generation Southern Baptist minister, in 2011; today it has nine hundred members and includes both rabbis and imams. Most of them have left their church positions, although a significant number continue to work in the church. A few, like Gretta Vosper, have told the truth about their loss of faith to their congregations. After losing a sizable portion of her flock, she began to attract new people. Her standing in the United Church of Canada was seriously threatened, but eventually the local jurisdiction agreed to allow her to continue to minister to her congregation under their banner. Asked by the *New York Times* about her commitment to continue in ministry, she said she has always understood God obliquely as love. Period.

What's New?

Actually, most of the critique by the New Atheists and the newly disillusioned ministers is not very new. Many of their objections had already been clearly enunciated in the eighteenth century by Hume. The nineteenth century gave us Friedrich Nietzsche's incisive and scathing attack on Christianity from several fronts, but probably most famously in his declaration that "God is dead." By this he meant that the Judeo-Christian conception of God is no longer able to speak to us. The world has changed, "come of age," in Dietrich Bonhoeffer's phrase, and we can no longer relate in any meaningful way to such a God. We have outgrown the notion of a heavenly father who creates us, sustains us, and cares about our welfare and our behavior.

The consequences of not facing up to this new situation, Nietzsche said, are not only intellectual dishonesty but extreme spiritual danger: we had lost the natural urge for self-affirmation. The primary drive of humankind, said Nietzsche, is the will to power. Christianity has tried to convince us that meekness is morally preferable, an obvious example of bad faith designed to enable the meek to feel good about themselves.

In the mid-twentieth century, a number of Christian theologians took Nietzsche's critique to heart and became known as the "God is dead" theologians, or "Christian atheists." The best known was Thomas J. J. Altizer. Unsurprisingly, they were widely misunderstood and chastised. A famous *Time* magazine cover from 1966 asked in large, red letters on a black background, "Is God Dead?" The reaction was loud and almost exclusively negative, even vituperative.

Meanwhile, a Lutheran pastor and theologian who had been executed by the Nazis in the 1940s was gaining more and more notice in the United States and Europe. Dietrich Bonhoeffer had been appalled at the pathetic resistance—and often nonresistance—the German churches had put up to counter the rise of the Nazis, and he became involved in an anti-Hitler group that eventually plotted to assassinate the führer. Sitting in his cell prior to his execution, he wrote letters to a dear friend and entries in his notebook describing the religionless age at which we had arrived and calling for a "religionless Christianity" to evolve to meet the times.

He wrote, "What is bothering me incessantly is the question what Christianity really is, or indeed who Christ really is, for us today. The time when people could be told everything by means of words, whether theological or pious, is over, and so is the time of inwardness and conscience—and that means the time of religion in general. We are moving toward a completely religionless time; people as they are now simply cannot be religious anymore."[1]

Rudolf Bultmann and his followers had set forth a "demythologized" interpretation of Christian biblical theology, reinterpreting the gospel in terms of its relevance to human existence. Bonhoeffer welcomed Bultmann's demythologizing but thought the problem went much deeper. Beyond outmoded statements of belief, whether biblical or doctrinal, was the fact that in a world in which Christians could so readily adapt to Nazism, even the traditional notions of inwardness and Christian conscience were suspect.

The thesis laid out in the following chapters is that a Christian worldview and a Christian-inspired life are possible—indeed, more empowering—without either the "beliefs" or the otherworldliness of conventional orthodoxy. In addition to revisiting the still somewhat explosive views of Bultmann, Altizer, and Bonhoeffer, we will also ask a more contemporary question: "So what? Why should I care? I'm living my life just fine—better, in fact—without the spirituality or religious accoutrements of Christianity." Among the 23 percent of Americans who claim no religion, there are no doubt some who, like the New Atheists, are intellectually offended by the irrationality of Christian doctrine. But I would guess there are many more who simply have no interest in the question. We will discuss this in a separate chapter—and throughout the remainder of the book.

WHAT IS LEFT?

Without the mythology and otherworldliness, what, if anything, is left of Christian faith? Are there alternative ways to access the worldview and spirituality of Christianity? If there are, why would anyone want to do that? Maybe we should just close all the church doors (several are closing at this moment), admit that Christianity is passé, and have the courage to create meaning for ourselves out of the void.

The answer that someone with my background might be expected to give is that, despite our inability to accept the doctrines of Christianity, we still find ourselves comforted by the Christian worldview and spirituality and by being part of a community of like-minded people. If that sounds like wish fulfillment, it's because in many cases it probably is.

That is not my case. I always have to smile when I read Freud's critique of religion as wish fulfillment. I think, "Are you kidding? I wouldn't 'wish for'

Christianity on a bet unless I couldn't find any way to avoid it." If I were to try to come up with a wish I'd like to fulfill, I hope I could do better than pick a path that requires me to "turn" from much of my ordinary life and count all my accomplishments as rubbish (or, in David Bentley Hart's New Testament translation, excrement), asks a rich young man to sell all he has and give the proceeds to the poor, and carries with it never-ending, intermittent doubt. To top it off, the founder spends his last day on earth hanging in agony from a cross. It's not a wish that springs immediately to mind.

My friend Danny says, "Hold it. Freud thought it was the wish for a life in heaven after death that was the draw." I respond, "That's very questionable as a 'Christian' belief. Nearly all the biblical references to a general resurrection have to do with an event that supposedly occurs simultaneously for everyone 'at the close of the age.' Many Christians today wouldn't bet the farm on a literal interpretation of that."

Danny says, "Be that as it may, most people who call themselves 'Christian' do think we pass on immediately to an afterlife, and it's those people Freud is talking about."

Point taken, but again, that's not my case. And this is all about me—unless maybe it's also about you.

So even if—for me—it's a stony path, isn't the Christian message supposed to ultimately be "good news?" Well, yes, but the key word is *ultimately*. The only authentic reason, in my view, to follow the Christian path is that you find it transformative. What that means exactly will be the subject of our exploration.

Too Radical?

But Danny wonders whether my view of the gospel isn't "radical." "Count all my accomplishments as excrement? Really? Who wants that? And what in heaven for?" My answer is that, like it or not, Jesus was radical, and although some branches of Christianity have spent many centuries trying to transform his image into Mr. Moderate Nice Guy, he certainly wasn't that. More to the point, Danny's right; you wouldn't casually choose the gospel path, as most people in first-century Judea and Asia Minor did not. You'd have to be knocked off your horse.

Many Paths

It is my belief that there are not one but several routes into the Christian message that are still able to speak meaningfully, even transformatively, to many Christians, as well as those outside the church. For the most part, these paths have been there since the beginning of the church, eventually obscured by the development of "orthodox" doctrine and dogma.

Of course, for many people, none of these alternative paths will inspire. As the word *inspire* implies, many will not be able or willing to "breathe them in." And it is the "breathing in," rather than the recitation of doctrine, that is the essence of Christianity.

That there may, however, be a willing audience for one or more of these alternative, nonmythological paths to the heart of Christianity is supported by the recent Western fascination with Buddhism. Buddhism is a religion that, in its oldest and purest form, does away with theistic mythology altogether and simply outlines four truths about the ubiquity of suffering and a "noble pathway" to walk in light of those truths.

It is also a sign of a new openness to Bonhoeffer's "religionless Christianity" that many people now call themselves "spiritual but not religious." Will some of these "spiritual but not religious" people, as well as some totally nonspiritual, nonreligious people and some doubting Christians, find anything in the following chapters that they can "breathe in?" I believe so. I have.

But of course, not all will. For starters, the New Atheists are surely correct that for many Christians and other religious adherents, religion is tribal. Contrary to being put off by the language of beliefs and creeds, they appear to find comfort in buying into the same belief system as others in their cohort.

For many others, Christian beliefs may not be central to their Christian experience or Christian lives, but they employ the language of doctrine for the same reason they employ English or French: it's the language they have learned. This group may find it confusing when they realize at some point in their spiritual development, often in college, that the language of doctrines and creeds is a dead language.

For this latter group, and increasingly for some more self-aware Christians, the power of Christianity in their lives is better expressed in a very different language, if indeed it is expressed in language at all. More likely, their faith is based on strong feelings, intuitions, visions, a sense of community, felt commitments and an unexpected power to act on them. For our purposes, however, we will try to unpack these visions and commitments into *language*, for an obvious reason: so we can talk about them. We will use this method to look at four of these paths into Christian faith.

But before we can do that, we must set the stage.

First of all, we must address the "So what?" question. Why should anyone today care about religion, particularly a religion based on events that occurred two thousand years ago? Chapter 1 will try to speak to this question.

Second, we will need to understand how we came to misrepresent the Christian message so badly. Chapter 2 will ask, How is it that a religion that claims to be based on "revelation" could end up being understood by adherents and opponents alike as being based on believing unbelievable statements? We will attempt to understand how this happened.

In chapter 3, we will look at how each of these paths makes an assumption that those outside the church, particularly those in the "So what?" group as well as many Christians, may not be willing to grant: *There is something wrong with you.* There is, in fact, something wrong with the whole finite world. It needs correcting. *You* need correcting. You and I need healing. If you do not share this assumption, none of these paths will appeal to you or, indeed, make any sense to you. So we will spend a bit of time discussing what it is that Christians feel is wrong with them, with us.

In chapter 4, we will come to grips with some basic terms we will need in our discussion of faith. We will ask, What is a religion? What is an atheist? What is a Christian atheist? What would Bonhoeffer's "religion-less Christianity" look like? What is a religious experience? What is "the holy"? What do we really know about the historical Jesus? Is the language of Christian existentialism passé?

Finally, before taking a look at our four alternative paths, chapter 5 will examine some interesting recent writing on the connection between "God" and "good."

Then, at last, we will attempt to capture the spirit of each of the four paths.

The overriding theme of the first three Gospels—Matthew, Mark, and Luke—is the prophetic proclamation of a man, Jesus of Nazareth, that "the kingdom of God is at hand." So in chapter 6, we will ask, What if the question of faith was not "Do you believe in God?" but rather "Do you believe in (trust in) Jesus's vision of the *kingdom* of God, and do you find it transformative?"

In chapter 7, we will look at the so-called Holy Spirit and what it means to be guided by it. We will ask, What if the question of faith was not "Do you believe in God?" but rather "Do you believe in (trust in) a path of ongoing and evolving spiritual inspiration?"

Chapter 8 will look at the notion of grace. Jesus's proclamation was not only that the kingdom of God is at hand but that we corrupt people are given the gift of being able to enter it if we "turn." That is, in fact, what Jesus says is the "good news," or gospel. So we will ask, What if the question of faith was not "Do you believe in God?" but rather "Are you astonished to find yourself accepted, even empowered, despite your knowledge that there is something wrong with you? Are you able to accept that acceptance?"

In chapter 9, we will look at Paul's notion of "Christ in you." Many Christians are motivated and inspired by this semimystical vision of the Christ within themselves. We will ask, What if the question of faith was not "Do you believe in God?" but rather "Do you believe in (trust in) the possibility of being transformed by uncovering the Christ within you?"

In chapter 10, we will attempt to "bring it all back home." Literally.

"There is no God, and Mary is his mother" is a quotation attributed for decades to George Santayana, an American philosopher from the turn of the twentieth century. Santayana was a radical skeptic who nevertheless continued to find the Catholic mass a source of profound inspiration. More recently, unable to find a place where Santayana actually made this statement, scholars have speculated that it was in fact said by the poet Robert Lowell as a mocking parody of Santayana's position. Santayana is probably smiling somewhere.

1

SO WHAT?

Why should I care about Christianity or the Christian life? Why should anybody? Who needs it? After all, it's a full life. There are adventures to be had, relationships to form, kids to raise, careers to build, and much, much more. That's enough, isn't it?

For an increasing number of people with a philosophical turn of mind, the response is, "Why religion indeed?" For even more people, it's not even a question. The subject isn't even on their screens.

As it happens, there has been a spate of books in recent decades about the supposed "plus side" of Christianity, books that concede that Christianity as a religion is outmoded but argue that it still has some other usefulness for individuals and society.

Often these books find *ethical* value in the teachings of Jesus: the Golden Rule, love and justice for all, humility, forgiveness, and so forth. In his book *Living the*

Secular Life, Phil Zuckerman says that most contemporary secular people live by the Golden Rule: treat others as you would like to be treated. In fact, he calls it the bedrock of secular morality. He also points out, correctly, that some variant of it occurs in many ancient texts from several different religions and secular sources. None of these versions, he says, requires a God; they just require basic, human empathy.

Harvey Cox, a professor of theology at Harvard Divinity School, for many years taught a popular course for undergraduates called Jesus and the Moral Life, and he has written about it in his book *When Jesus Came to Harvard: Making Moral Choices Today*. The book and the course are not a rejection of Christianity as a religion, although Cox has a nuanced view of that looming possibility and doesn't find it distressing, but they do emphasize the moral dimension of Christianity. Cox uses the life and teachings of Jesus as a way to challenge his students to consider the moral issues of our day and, more importantly, to reflect on what it means to reason morally and what the implications are for moral conviction and moral courage.

Another nuanced view of Christianity's supposed "plus side" is that of French philosopher André Comte-Sponville in his charming and beautifully written book *The Little Book of Atheist Spirituality*. Comte-Sponville was raised Roman Catholic and lost his faith at the age of eighteen. However, he affirms his personal religious history, as well as the Judeo-Christian history of the Western world, for creating and instilling what are—with horrible, historical exceptions, of course—humane values, such as honesty, courage, generosity, gentleness, compassion, justice, and love. He simply thinks these values can be maintained and passed on without any reference to God. He therefore calls himself a "faithful atheist."

Zuckerman, Cox, and Comte-Sponville are surely right that Christianity has moral and cultural value, but that is not what this book is about.

Rather, it is about how Christianity can still have *spiritual* value and the power to transform lives, power that inspires us to not only live morally but also face the anxiety of being an existing human being and search for ways to make that transformation real in the real world.

Christianity has always had to reinvent itself, and it always will. That is the so-called Protestant principle. And perhaps Christianity is on the verge of reinventing itself as something not explicitly "Christian," something in which the historical figure of Jesus plays a minor or even nonexistent role. That remains to be seen. But the response of this book to the question "Why should we care?" is this: we should care because we are human beings, and something inside us—or inside some of us, anyway—seeks healing and transformation and some sort of reconciliation.

As it happens, there are two recent books outside the Christian tradition that come closer to our thread. They have little in common with each other except that they both make us wonder if we are "hardwired" in a way that often expresses itself religiously.

Robert Wright's thought-provoking book *Why Buddhism Is True* argues that the Buddha's diagnosis of the human condition reflects the psychological evolution of the human species. Natural selection, Wright says, has "designed" the human brain in a way that misleads us and enslaves us. The "goal" of natural selection is to get our genes into the next generation, and the most efficient way to do that is to delude us into thinking that the pleasures of life will not fade. We throw ourselves unreservedly into eating, having sex, impressing our peers, and beating out our rivals because the subset of people in prior generations who were genetically predisposed to pursue these goals had the best shot at passing on their genes.

The Buddha taught us that the underlying principle of our pursuit of pleasure—that it will not fade—is an illusion. Living a life of pleasure will always disappoint us because the unbridled pursuit of pleasure inevitably leads to pain, whether it be ennui or obesity or anxiety or addiction or guilt or a sense of meaninglessness or some other form of alienation. The Buddha teaches us to liberate ourselves from the illusion that pleasure will not have a price—through mindfulness, arrived at by meditation. When we become clear that we are not in charge of our own behavior, we can let go and achieve self-realization or, in more Buddhist terms, realize that we are "not-self." As Wright says, the truth of both Buddhism and evolutionary psychology is that our CEO is MIA: we are not in charge.

So Wright's answer to the question of why we should care about Buddhism is that we are hardwired for self-destruction and Buddhist practices offer a path to transcend that wiring. In chapter 3, "What is Wrong with You? (If Anything)," we will look at the Christian correlate of the Buddha's vision.

Another extraordinary account of hardwiring is Jill Bolte Taylor's *My Stroke of Insight* as well as her TED talk based on the same events. The book is good, but the YouTube video of the TED talk is mind-blowing. It is not surprising that at one point it was the second most-viewed TED talk of all time.[1]

In December of 1996, Dr. Taylor, a neuroanatomist working at Harvard's brain research center, woke up to find herself in the throes of a massive stroke. The left hemisphere of her brain shut down, leaving her unable to walk, talk, read, write, or recall anything from her life. Instead, she experienced only the functioning of her right brain.

The right brain, she explains, experiences only *this moment* and all that is going on in it: sights, sounds, smells, all the information of our senses, in one holistic experience. It thinks in pictures and knows itself as an "energy-being," connected to every other energy-being in the universe. In the right brain, we are the entire human family, and we are "perfect, whole, and beautiful."

The left brain, by contrast, thinks methodically and linearly. Its concern is not the present moment; its concern is how to connect the present moment to the past and future. The left brain takes the right brain's picture of *Now!*, picks out details, organizes all the information, and tries to connect it to everything in the past we have ever learned and project it onto the future. Most importantly, it says, "I am. I am an individual, contained in a particular body, and not just a flood of energy that flows into all the other energy in the universe."

As her left brain shut down to nearly zero, she realized that she was no longer the choreographer of her life, and she knew, This is Nirvana! I am still alive, and I am in Nirvana! And if I can step to the right of my left brain and experience the overwhelmingly beautiful euphoria of Nirvana, everyone can do it!

Perhaps there are connections here to Christian experience. Can the vision of the "kingdom of God," for example, or "eternal life" be right-brain phenomena and the creeds and other "beliefs" left-brain interpretations? Could it be that hardwiring for religious experience resides in the separation of the two hemispheres of our brains? Could it be that the answer to the question of why we should care about religion is that we are hardwired for it? If religion, as anthropologists once thought, is a "cultural universal," our hardwired brains could be a possible explanation.

In a 1970s interview with the BBC, the Black civil rights icon, theologian, and university pastor Howard Thurman put it this way: "Religious experience is dynamic, fluid, effervescent, yeasty. But the mind [left brain?] can't handle these, so it has to imprison religious experience in some way, get it all bottled up. Then when the experience quiets down, the mind draws a bead on it and extracts concepts, notions, dogmas, so that religious experience can make sense to the mind."[2]

Why should we care about Christianity, even a "religionless" Christianity? Wright, Taylor, and Thurman each in their own way speak of an innate, human dimension, a spiritual dimension, that is fundamental to our existence. Their experiences and observations transcend orthodox religion while remaining recognizably grounded in it. Wright and Taylor connect their experiences and observations to Theravada Buddhism (which, interestingly enough, is often described as a "religionless religion" because it makes no reference to a god). Thurman traces Christian doctrine to its spiritual roots in human experience. These are three responses to the question of "so what—why should we care?" They also hint at a partial answer to our question of what a religionless Christianity might look like.

2

HOW DID WE SCREW THIS UP SO BADLY?

First of all, let's concede that for probably the majority of Christians, Christianity didn't screw this up at all. Many appear to be perfectly happy with the creeds—those official summaries of Christian doctrine, arrived at by councils of bishops in the early church—and other mainstream Christian beliefs. It is mostly the intellectuals who have been turned off. (I'll leave out of this account, for now, the reportedly even larger subgroup of the "So Whats," people who just stopped caring one way or the other about religion.)

Second, before we exclusively blame the creeds, let's concede that even the first three Gospels, as they appear in the Bible, already contain, in addition to the story, a great deal of analysis and interpretation of the meaning of Jesus's life, and it is reasonable to assume that strands of the oral tradition must also have contained substantial interpretation. Most mainstream scholars believe that it was the disciples' uncanny experiences of the living presence of Jesus after his death that changed the narrative from the "Jesus of history" to "the Christ of faith," as Martin Kähler called it. And with that change came interpretation and "beliefs."

A QUICK OVERVIEW OF THE HISTORY OF ORTHODOX DOCTRINE AND DOGMA

Already, by the time the Gospels were written, Jesus was no longer simply the prophet of the coming kingdom of God but rather "the Messiah" (anointed one, *Christos* in Greek) of Jewish expectation, the "Son of God," the "Risen One," or the one who was expected to return at the dawn of the new age. Other, more exotic beliefs came about to try to make sense of Jesus's special status. He was believed to have been conceived in the union of a young virgin and the Holy Spirit. He had supernatural powers and could interfere with nature by calming seas or expanding the on-hand supply of bread. (The healing "miracles" are a special case and will be discussed later.)

There had been plenty of time for these interpretations and beliefs to arise and develop. The first Gospel account to be written, Mark's, did not appear in its biblical form until probably 66 to 70 CE, over thirty-five years after the events it professes to recount. During that time, various strands of oral tradition had been evolving. After Mark brought his oral sources together and wrote the story down, his Gospel was read and used as a source by both Matthew and Luke. The two of them almost certainly used another common source, a collection of Jesus's sayings, that has never been found and that scholars call simply "Q" (for *Quelle*, the German word for "source"). It is for these reasons we speak of the first three Gospels together; they are the "synoptic" Gospels, meaning they share a point of view.

In any event, after the Easter experiences—whatever we are to make of them—Jesus's followers began to develop "beliefs" about his status and significance, and these beliefs are already represented in the synoptic Gospels.

The author of the fourth Gospel, John, and the apostle Paul greatly expanded the mythology of the new community. For John, Christ was a preexisting figure who had come to earth to lead us into eternal life. John sounds like a theologian. And Paul made Christ part of a cosmic drama in which the first Adam brought about sin and death while Christ, the "second Adam," overcame them both with his sacrificial death.

In Egypt and elsewhere, various Gnostic communities, some of them identifying as Christian, developed.

These communities claimed mystical access to secret knowledge (*gnosis*), and Christian Gnostics produced their own gospels with names like the *Gospel of Thomas*, the *Gospel of Mary Magdalene*, the *Gospel of Mary*, the *Gospel of Philip*, and the *Gospel of Truth*. Some of them preserved a few of the traditions found in the synoptic Gospels, but some of them did not, and they all varied in significant ways from the Synoptics, as well as from John and Paul. The Gnostic gospels emphasize acquiring spiritual enlightenment rather than being saved from sin. Their cosmology posits an evil demiurge, or half-god, as the creator of the material world, thus discarding the benevolent, creator God of the Old Testament who pronounced his creation good. The Gnostic gospels are also more likely to honor feminine spirituality and mythology. And they grant enlightened persons the same status as Christ himself. In brief, they often sound more like Hinduism than emerging orthodox Christianity. (Some scholars have even explored the possibility that one of the apostles—Thomas is the usual suspect—may have visited India and been exposed to the Hindu scriptures.)

I remember that Danny and I were both enthralled by the Gnostics we read about in Tillich's course on the religions and philosophies of the Hellenistic period. It was 1960, and although we didn't know it yet, it was the predawn of the Age of Aquarius. Zen Buddhism was being taught at Harvard, of all places. Four years later, we'd both be living with our wives in Woodstock, New York, where our neighbor Bob Dylan was about to announce that the times were a-changin', and Timothy Leary in nearby Millbrook was telling the world that LSD was revelatory.

Elaine Pagels, Karen King, and other scholars now consider the Gnostic gospels to be sources that add to the richness of Christianity, but early Christian writers like Irenaeus and Tertullian found them threatening and insisted on stamping out the Gnostic beliefs and reemphasizing the beliefs of the developing biblical canon and the emerging mainstream tradition.

The formal, official creeds did not follow until the fourth century. The emperor Constantine, after his conversion to Christianity, gathered the Council of Nicaea in 325 CE. At that time, the problem, as Constantine saw it, was that there were several versions of the Christian message circulating in the Roman Empire and beyond. He was concerned, not about the Gnostics, but about controversies among those who each claimed to represent the orthodox point of view, and he felt it his duty as head of the empire to resolve the conflicts and present a unified understanding of the faith to its new Roman adherents. In particular, he insisted on resolving one outstanding issue: the so-called Arian controversy.

Arius was a presbyter, a church leader, in Alexandria who taught that, although Jesus was the "Son of God," he came into being at a particular point in time as the first and most perfect of the Father's creatures. Unlike God the Father, there was a time when the Son didn't exist, and he was therefore in some sense subordinate to the Father. Arius's view had become popular in many circles and was the source of a major, disruptive controversy in the church. The bishops at the Council of Nicaea ruled that Jesus Christ was of one substance (*homoousios*) with the Father and declared Arius a heretic. This may sound like much ado about nothing today, but many Christian denominations down to the present moment recite the Nicene Creed every Sunday, including the clause that says that Jesus Christ is of one substance with the Father (usually translated today as "of one Being with the Father").

Other councils laid down dogma regarding such pressing metaphysical questions as whether Christ had one nature (a sort of dilute mixture of divine and human) or two. (The answer, according to the Council of Chalcedon: Christ was both fully divine and fully human, but his two natures were united in one *hypostasis*, or underlying reality.) Huh?

In fairness, the questions raised at the councils were not for mere idle speculation. The bishops were no doubt aware that their creedal formulas had implications for religious *practice*. Popular piety of the day included the felt urge to pray directly to Jesus Christ. Such prayer would have been blasphemous if directed toward a half-god who was not "true God from true God" (Nicaea) or was part-divine, part-human (rejected at Chalcedon).

THE DOGMA QUESTIONED

At the turn of the twentieth century, German scholar Adolf von Harnack protested that the creeds had taken Christianity down a strange, foreign path. They had been created—as, to a lesser extent, had the theologies of John and Paul—outside the Jewish context of the actual life of Jesus. The creeds had been greatly influenced by the Hellenistic philosophies of the day, employing concepts such as substance and hypostases that were alien to the original Jewish-Christian message. Harnack's goal was to uncover the "nub" of Christianity. His answer to the question "How did we screw this up so badly?" was that we had made Christianity into a dogmatic belief in metaphysical statements that later became impossible to believe. So far, that would seem to be our theme as well.

But Paul Tillich, while he was no fan of this sort of antiquated dogma, was skeptical that the Hellenistic conceptualization of Christianity either could have or should have been prevented or that there was ever a "nub" of Christianity to uncover. To Tillich, the creeds, as well as the biblical titles given to Jesus, were not a hideous error but the inevitable outcome of people's need to understand the phenomenon of Jesus. And Tillich also thought that Christianity needed to be constantly reinterpreted for each new historical moment, and for him that meant, in our time, the language of existentialism—that is, the language of *subjective human experience*—rather than the language of science or history or objective fact.

For Tillich, faith did not mean acceptance of beliefs but rather "ultimate concern." Whatever concerns us ultimately is what we can be said to have faith or trust in. Some may come to the Christian faith via one of the Christian paths we will be exploring. But one may also have ultimate trust in the "American way" or the vision of Karl Marx or the expansion of scientific knowledge or, indeed, our own self-glorification. The line between "believers" and "nonbelievers" is erased. The question is no longer how anyone could possibly believe in a non-scientific metaphysics; but rather, given the existential demand to choose where we will place our trust, the question is, On what worldview—whether Christian or non-Christian, whether religious or secular—are we willing to stake the meaning of our lives?

Why "ultimate *concern*"? "Concern" seems like a weak word; why not "ultimate conviction?" Tillich recognized that doubt is part of the deal. Doubt isn't the opposite of faith; it's part of faith. Faith is the never-ending struggle of trust overcoming doubt. (Or not. But then it's no longer faith.) The constant factor in the wrestling of faith and doubt is concern. To say that something concerns us ultimately is to say, "Either my trust in *this* is affirmed, or else I must admit that I ultimately trust in nothing." The opposite of faith is despair.

It will be Tillich and one of his principal influences, Søren Kierkegaard, on whom we will mainly rely to show us the way to a nonmythological, existentialist understanding of religion.

Surprisingly, "New Atheist" Sam Harris explicitly excludes Tillich from his analysis of the foolishness of Christian beliefs on the grounds that Tillich's approach is way out of the mainstream, an odd comment on the work of a man generally recognized, along with Karl Barth, as one of the two most important Protestant theologians of the twentieth century. The exclusion apparently reflects Harris's correct assessment that Tillich's work isn't easily dismissed as unscientific, metaphysical beliefs.

So the answer to the question of how we got to our current dead end of Christian faith as the believing of the unbelievable is twofold. For those denominations that define Christianity by the ancient creeds—especially, but not exclusively, the Roman Catholic Church—the language of those creeds has become, for many, irrelevant, even incomprehensible, in the modern world.

In the less creed-based churches—especially, but not exclusively, the evangelical and fundamentalist churches—it is the doctrines contained in the New Testament itself, such as the supernaturalism of Jesus or the literal end of history and the advent of the new age or the physical resurrection of the dead or the pre-existence of the Son or his sacrifice for our sins, that are the stumbling blocks to faith for increasing numbers of people.

But some who have found it impossible to relate to either of these traditional paths have discovered a more contemporary faith: not a compendium of statements we are asked to believe, but an affirmation of our ultimate concern and an acceptance of the power to live it out.

3

WHAT'S WRONG WITH YOU? (IF ANYTHING)

If you don't think anything is wrong with you or your world, Christianity is probably not for you. You can't be healed from a condition you don't have. Christianity shouldn't judge you for this. Jesus himself said that those who are well have no need of a physician and that the message was for "those who have ears to hear." (Or are these two sayings incompatible with each other? Is there a judgment implied in the idea that some may not have ears to hear? It's hard to say.)

In any case, what is it that Christians think is wrong with us? What is it we feel a need to be healed from?

A look at today's newspaper makes many of us feel that something is seriously out of whack with humanity as a whole. The early twentieth-century British wit G. K. Chesterton said it is odd that some people have rejected the doctrine of original sin (the doctrine that we are all born sinners) because it is the only doctrine that can be empirically verified.

Many others of us look into our own hearts and see a shadow there. We know that, despite our best intentions, we often mistreat others, sometimes in very ugly ways.

My friend Danny thinks this would be a good place to make an example of myself and discuss my own sinfulness. I say, "*You* make an example of *your*self, buddy!" Actually, I do get into that a bit in chapter 9, but this stuff is always ambiguous, and we have to remember—before oversharing—what Anne Lamott's father told her: The first commandment is "Don't be an asshole."[1]

What's Wrong with Us, According to the Hebrew Bible?

The answer has varied a bit over the centuries, at least in emphasis. In both testaments of the Bible, the principal thing that's wrong with us is, of course, sin. If you were with me up to now, I may have just lost you. Sin has certainly gotten a bad name, so to speak, in recent years, but in case you are one of those who have ears to hear, hang in there for a moment. You may have a fundamentalist, or perhaps a medieval, idea of sin, of which I will try to disabuse you. Here's a working definition: Tillich translates *sin* as "alienation," meaning alienation from God, from our deepest and truest selves, from our ultimate concern. (This is not a forced translation. The Greek word usually translated as "sin" [*hamartia*] literally means "missing the mark.") Tillich also tells us that we should speak not of *sins* but only of *sin*—our total existential alienation from what is ultimate rather than an unhelpful catalog of the various ways in which that alienation may manifest itself.

Already in the Hebrew Bible, the Christian Old Testament, sin has layers of meaning. Throughout much of the Old Testament, sin is collective. It describes the sins of the people of Israel. Often it refers to idolatry—literally, the worship of idols, a violation of the second commandment, "You shall not make for yourself an idol," but more symbolically, a violation of the first commandment, "You shall [as a people] have no other gods before me." In existential terms, God demands that Israel not treat as ultimate anything that is not worthy of their ultimate concern. That demand is vague and probably not terribly helpful to skeptical readers, but it at least avoids the archaic language that we are trying to reinterpret while internalizing the Old Testament's assessment of what is wrong with us: in our fallen, alienated state, we choose to center our common life around the trivial, the corrupt, the unholy.

The prophet Amos emphasizes that our alienation from God's law leads us into systemic injustice as he dramatically calls out the exploiters of the poor: "Hear this, you that trample on the needy, and bring to ruin the poor of the land, saying, 'When will the new moon be over so that we may sell grain; and the sabbath, so that we may offer wheat for sale? We will make the ephah small and the shekel great, and practice deceit with false balances, buying the poor for silver and the needy for a pair of sandals, and selling the sweepings of the wheat'" (Amos 8:4–6).

The prophet Jeremiah finds that the cure for our alienation lies in the healing of the human heart: "This is the covenant that I will make with the house of Israel after those days, says the Lord: I will put my law within them, and I will write it on their hearts; and I will be their God, and they shall be my people. No longer shall they teach one another, or say to each other, 'Know the Lord,' for they shall all know me, from the least of them to the greatest, says the Lord; for I will forgive their iniquity, and remember their sin no more" (Jer 31:33–34).

And the prophet Micah adds, "He has told you, O mortal, what is good; and what does the Lord require of you but to do justice, and to love kindness, and to walk humbly with your God?" (Mic 6:8).

These last two passages do not need to be translated into existentialist language; they are already in existentialist language, the language of subjective human experience. The good lives in the human heart and includes the demand for justice, kindness, and humility. *That we are alienated from these goods, that they do not come naturally to us, is in large part what is wrong with us.*

What's Wrong with You, According to the New Testament?

Jesus's interpretation of sin, as portrayed in the synoptic Gospels, is often misunderstood as replacing the law and the prophets with a gospel of love. But Jesus was from birth to death a religious Jew, and in the Sermon on the Mount, he explicitly states that he is not preaching replacement of the law. Rather, as the Jewish scholar Geza Vermes puts it, Jesus is aiming to renew the law internally by stressing its spiritual significance. Thus, "You have heard that it was said to those of ancient times, 'You shall not murder.' . . . But I say to you that if you are angry with a brother or sister, you will be liable to judgment" (Matt 5:21a, 22a). Likewise, because lust is the root of adultery, lusting amounts to committing adultery in your heart. *What is wrong with you is that you are alienated from the holy at your very roots.*

The way out, Jesus says, is a radical *kenosis*, or self-emptying. Instead of retaliating against an evildoer, we should resist the temptation to respond in kind; as Jesus put it, we should "turn the other cheek." Instead of loving our neighbor and hating our enemy, we should love our enemies and pray for those who persecute us. Why? Because if you love only those who love you, you're no different from anyone else. Even "Gentiles and tax-collectors" (Luke says "sinners") do good to those who do good to them. Your standard should be to act as the child of your Father in heaven that you are, and your Father makes his sun rise on the evil and the good and sends rain on the righteous and the unrighteous. For Jesus, the root of sin or alienation lies precisely in thinking with pride that there is nothing wrong with us because we are just like everybody else (Matt 5:46–47). We *are*, of course, just like the Gentiles and the tax-collectors, but that is the problem, not the solution.

In the Beatitudes that introduce the Sermon on the Mount, Jesus spells out the sort of self-emptying—of pride and self-centeredness—that is required of us to overcome our alienation. Blessed are the poor in spirit (in Luke, simply "the poor.") Blessed also are the meek, the merciful, the pure in heart, the peace-makers. A major part of what is wrong with us, according to Jesus, is our alienation from the king-dom of God and its path of "emptying" ourselves, a path of self-sacrificing love.

But something else is wrong with us as well. We are doomed to death (and a seemingly meaningless death at that). We can read this indirectly in the Gospels in the value Jesus places on eternal *life*. The Synoptics do not use the expression "eternal life" often. Mark puts it in the mouth of Jesus only twice. Matthew and Luke have parallel passages plus one other. The Gospel of John, the least historical of the Gospels, contains many instances of the phrase, both in the author's own voice and in that of Jesus. In some passages, it sounds synonymous with "abundant life." For example, in many passages, Jesus has come into the world to bring us eternal life; in John 10:10, he has come "that they may have life, and have it abundantly." *Part of what is wrong with us is that we do not live abundantly.*

In the Gospel of John, death is related to sin and alienation: "Very truly, I tell you, anyone who hears my word and believes him who sent me *has* eternal life, and does not come under judgment, but has passed from death to life" (John 5:24; emphasis mine).

And what exactly is eternal life? John has Jesus say, "*This* is eternal life, that they may know you, the only true God, and Jesus Christ whom you have sent" (John 17:3; emphasis mine). Eternal life in this passage is clearly something that happens now, not in some endless future (although there are hints of that in John as well). John contrasts eternal life with normal life "in this world." He quotes Jesus as saying, "Those who love their life lose it, and those who hate their life in this world will keep it for eternal life" (John 12:25). *There is indeed something wrong with you. You need to get out of here.*

As we will see, existentialists like Søren Kierkegaard and Paul Tillich also understand eternal life nonmythologically. For them, the symbol eternal life does not refer to life extended forever in a "better place," but rather to life lived *sub specie aeternitatis*, life from the perspective of "the eternal." What this could possibly mean is obviously unclear, but for now, suffice it to say that this mysterious idea is woven through all the paths we will look at. It is the symbol that reflects the felt ultimacy of these visions; that is, they are not finite—they are eternal. It is also the symbol that one of the things wrong with the world is the obvious challenge to "eternal life," namely, death.

WHAT'S WRONG WITH YOU, ACCORDING TO THE EXISTENTIALISTS?

To jump ahead then to the modern world: the nineteenth-century Danish philosopher and religious thinker Søren Kierkegaard saw what is wrong with us through the modern lens of anxiety and despair. Kierkegaard is generally considered the father of existentialism because of his scathing critique of the German philosopher G. W. F. Hegel. Hegel had demonstrated, to his own satisfaction—and, to be fair, to the satisfaction of a huge number of followers as well—that the world is evolving toward an infinite end point, and its process of evolution moves onward and upward without anything *essentially* going wrong with it or even impeding it much. Sure, there is contradiction, negation, even—and especially—war in world history (which Hegel called "antitheses"), but they are essentially resolved in the creation of new "syntheses." In the words of Max Ehrmann's 1927 poem "Desiderata," "the universe is unfolding as it should."[2] Don't worry, be happy; God's in his heaven, all's right with the world. Hegel even equated this with the Christian message.

Kierkegaard observed that, while all this might be true according to the logical necessity of Hegel's system of world history, it is decidedly not true of the individual's subjective experience. Individuals have only finite freedom, and our reaction to the impulse to transcend our current situation is not to skate along with world history but rather, more often than not, to fall prey to extreme *angst*. Anxiety, he said, is the "dizziness of freedom" as we confront the boundlessness of possibilities. *What is wrong with us is that our alienation manifests itself in existential anxiety and despair.*

World history rolls on; whatever happens, happens; the resulting next stage does indeed seem foreordained. But individuals have to make *choices*: what to do next, who to be next, who or what to become. And in our finitude, while we can see that these choices are extremely high stakes, we can't see a clear path, and we experience vertigo—the dizziness of freedom.

According to Kierkegaard, "Anxiety is altogether different from fear and similar concepts that refer to something definite, whereas anxiety is freedom's actuality as the possibility of possibility."[3]

"All existence," Kierkegaard says, "makes me anxious, from the smallest fly to the mysteries of the Incarnation; the whole thing is inexplicable to me, I myself most of all; to me, all existence is infected."[4]

It would be tempting to dismiss Kierkegaard as neurotic, and there is plenty of evidence that he probably was. But as Tillich says, the anxieties that send us to therapists are caused by conflicts between various parts of our personality—for example, in Freudian theory, our unconscious drives versus repressive norms. The goal of therapy is to remove the anxiety. Existential anxiety, such as Kierkegaard is describing, cannot be removed, says Tillich; it can only be healed by the courage to affirm ourselves in spite of our anxiety—that is, by taking the anxiety into ourselves and facing it squarely.

This confrontation is not for everyone. Countless people experience anxiety, and many seek out mental health professionals. Many of them are helped. Some, however, feel the need, as Tillich says, for a "physician of souls," which, ironically, is the literal meaning of "psychiatrist." These people do not want their anxiety medicated or removed, and at some level, they know that it cannot be. They want, rather, to be given the "courage to be."

For Kierkegaard, the flip side of this existential anxiety is *despair*. Kierkegaard calls it "the sickness unto death." It results from the total failure of the spirit to move on and transcend its present situation, a total inability to choose what to do next, who to be, what to become. We find ourselves stuck in a prison of finitude, and our anxiety morphs into the perception that everything is ultimately pointless. Becoming indifferent is our way of resolving our anxiety, but the price is very high indeed. *What is wrong with us is that, left to our own self-centered devices, our alienation leads either to shallow everydayness or to anxiety and despair.*

Tillich, starting from Kierkegaard's analysis, breaks down our existential anxiety and despair a little further. Contra Hegel again, Tillich cites three forms of anxiety that threaten our self-affirmation. The first of these is the most basic because it is totally destructive of our very selves, it is universally felt, and it is inescapable. It is the anxiety of fate and death.

Death is absolute; fate is the more relative form of the same anxiety. Our basic affirmation of self is threatened by arbitrariness, unpredictability, and irrationality—what Karl Jaspers called "boundary situations." It appears unsolicited and unwanted in the form of weakness, disease, and accidents. In the New Testament period, it included the anxiety caused by the arbitrariness of having the fertile, religious culture of the Jews tightly circumscribed by the hegemony of the Roman Empire.

The second form of anxiety is what Tillich calls the anxiety of emptiness and meaninglessness. While it does not threaten our very being in the way that death does, the anxiety of meaninglessness threatens our *spiritual* self-affirmation. The anxiety of meaninglessness, Tillich says, is anxiety about the loss of an ultimate concern, of "a meaning that gives meaning to all meanings." It is experienced as the loss of a spiritual center. Emptiness, the relative form of this type of anxiety, stems from the fact that whatever gave us meaning yesterday no longer does. As we try one new strategy after another, we gradually give in to indifference or to fanatical self-assertiveness—what psychiatrist Erich Fromm called "an escape from freedom."

The third form of anxiety, according to Tillich, is the anxiety of guilt and condemnation. It is this anxiety that threatens our *moral* self-affirmation. On the one hand, we are responsible for what we have made—and will make—of ourselves. On the other hand, because we are finite and our freedom is finite, it is impossible for us to take total responsibility for what we become. We cannot pick and choose, however, which choices we are going to consider beyond our control. Any individual choice is in principle within our control. We are therefore guilty from the outset. As Kierkegaard says, before God you are always wrong. At the extreme, this anxiety is experienced as condemnation.

The inevitability of these three interrelated forms of anxiety yields the hopelessness that Kierkegaard called despair. As Tillich points out, the Stoics considered suicide a possible escape from existential anxiety, but for the person in despair, suicide is not a solution. It is merely a confirmation of hopelessness.

So what is wrong with us? From biblical times to the present, the Judeo-Christian answer has consistently centered on our alienation from what is ultimate. If you are well and feel no need to be healed of alienation, you will not find any of the above analyses germane to your situation. But many do feel this need to be healed. To the question of "So what? Why should we care about religion?" they answer that they feel morally inadequate, torn by anxiety about death or fate, and spiritually on the brink of meaninglessness or despair. Such people want to be healed.

In the end, one may consider people who feel such basic alienation and the need for healing delusional, or neurotic, or unbalanced, but for those who are most deeply in touch with the human situation, the need for healing is all too real.

The Christian diagnosis of our situation, from biblical times to now, is that something in our world and in our very selves is out of round, or at least in danger of becoming out of round. Not everyone experiences this vertigo. Thomas Carlyle famously said of Socrates that he was "at ease in Zion." But for those who are ill at ease in Zion, for those for whom everydayness is not enough, and especially for those for whom despair is threatening to become "the sickness unto death," the search for a cure is urgent.

4

SOME TERMINOLOGY AND SOME LOOSE ENDS

WHAT IS A RELIGION?

Santayana said, "Every living and healthy religion has a marked idiosyncrasy. Its power consists in its special and surprising message and in the bias which that revelation gives to life. The vistas it opens and the mysteries it propounds are another world to live in; and another world to live in—whether we expect ever to pass wholly over into it or no—is what we mean by having a religion."[1]

This definition is reminiscent of Jesus's vision of the "kingdom of God," which clearly gives a "bias to life" and describes "another world to live in." Santayana described himself as an atheist and was described by others as an "aesthetic Catholic," meaning that he rejected the dogma and moralizing of the church but loved what he called the poetic power that "vitalizes the mind." It is from this perspective that he sees religion as a revelation or vision of "another world to live in." Santayana did not see religion as irrational but rather as a *form* of reason that, along with art, is central to life. He thought that religion loses its way, however, "whenever its symbolic rightness is taken for scientific truth."[2]

In other words, there is no God, and Mary is his mother.

What Is an Atheist?

The word *atheist* comes with a great deal of emotional baggage, pro and con, but basically, an atheist is simply a person who disavows theism. So what is theism?

Theism, in its strict theological sense, is the worship of what Hinduism calls a god or gods "with form"—that is, a god who is, as Tillich says, a being alongside other beings.[3] That is to say, such a god is an object to us in the same way that every other being is an object to us. When we relate to the theistic God of Christianity—a being we can describe, who has qualities that make "him" different from us—we relate to someone who is roughly of the same type of thing that we are. "He" is certainly more important than other beings, and "his" qualities are greatly magnified, sometimes described as infinitely magnified, but "he" is recognizable as the same sort of actor we and other people are. "He" creates, "he" leads, "he" has a will; in short, to "him," *we* are objects. "He" is certainly not Thomas Aquinas's "being-itself" or Tillich's "God above God" or "the power of being." The idea of a theistic God, literally conceived, is what offends atheists, as well it should.

Conservative Christian commentators have long said that Tillich is himself an atheist, and in an important sense, that is exactly right. He is not a theist. But instead of no God, he prefers to talk about the "God above the God of theism" (a phrase we will unpack later), and he finds theological theism as repugnant and wrong as any atheist.

We should add that Tillich also recognizes a personalistic form of theism in which theistic language is used to symbolize the felt encounter and relationship we have with the divine. As long as it is recognized as symbolic and not a literal description of the way God "really is," this kind of theism has a legitimate place. Truth to tell, this sort of personalism is probably the most prevalent way that most Christians, including me, relate to God and Jesus on a day-to-day basis.

It has long been fashionable in highbrow Christian circles to arch one's brow over nineteenth-century personalistic theism, like the "friend" in the gospel hymn "What a Friend We Have in Jesus." Psychologists criticize it as childish ideation. The guardians of "high Christology" criticize it as demeaning of the divine. But Harvard theologian Harvey Cox isn't buying the critiques. He likes to envision Jesus as a friend who "gently forces people to look at life differently and maybe even to live it differently."[4]

And of course, Jesus himself related to the divine as Father. What an irony that the subject of this personal relationship got turned into the "first person of the Trinity."

What Is a Christian Atheist?

Of the so-called radical, "God-is-dead" theologians of the 1960s, the most famous—some would say notorious—by far was Thomas J. J. Altizer, who recently died at the age of ninety-one after decades of semiobscurity. His notoriety was due in part to the fact that he was willing to talk to the press and had a rather theatrical manner. He even appeared on Merv Griffin's popular afternoon talk show, where the audience reaction was so violent that the director closed the curtains and ordered the band to start playing. Afterward, Altizer found a crowd at the stage door, demanding his death. It was a time when 97 percent of American adults professed a "belief in God." One is left to wonder what sort of God this is who would approve of killing Professor Altizer, although this would not be unheard-of divine behavior in some strands of the Bible.

While atheism has become more acceptable in the United States than it was in 1966, a recent article in the *New Yorker* reported that large numbers of Americans still do not approve of atheists teaching their children, marrying into their families, or becoming president of the United States. And avowed atheists still cannot join the Masonic Lodge or the Boy Scouts.

Altizer summarized his "Christian atheist" position in a documentary for National Educational Television, the precursor of PBS: The God of theism is no longer manifest, no longer "real." In short, we can no longer relate to a transcendent God who resides in heaven.

There are several ironies and apparent ironies in the story of Professor Altizer. As the *New York Times* obituary points out, he so angered and scandalized Christian evangelicals that he may well have helped give rise to the religious right. Scores of evangelicals attempted unsuccessfully to get him fired from his position at Emory University, one of the first in a long series of political actions that came to characterize the Christian right.

An apparent irony lies in the fact that Altizer fleshed out his theology of the death of God with what appears to be another theistic "belief": that God died when he became incarnate in Jesus Christ. Altizer probably meant only that the transcendent God was dead but that the immanent God was very much alive in our experience of Jesus Christ.

The importance of this movement to our understanding of Christianity lies in the abandonment of the notion that "atheist" and "religious" are opposites. One can be both. Like Santayana, Christian atheists feel Christianity is symbolically right and scientifically invalid. What criteria one would use to choose Christianity—if not objective, scientific truth—is, of course, the looming question.

What Would Bonhoeffer's "Religionless Christianity" Look Like?

Over twenty years prior to the God-is-dead movement in the United States, Dietrich Bonhoeffer sat in a solitary cell in Tegel Prison in Nazi Germany pondering how Christianity might confront a religionless world.

While many German churches had declared themselves Reich churches and sworn allegiance to Hitler, Bonhoeffer had started an alternative, underground seminary. At one point, he had accepted an invitation to teach at Union Seminary in New York, an invitation extended to get him out of Nazi Germany. But he soon felt a duty to return to his own country and bear witness to what he saw as the genuine Christian message.

Now he was in prison, prior to being executed for his apparent involvement in a failed plot to assassinate Hitler. In a 1944 letter to his dear friend Eberhard Bethge, he asked whether, in a religionless world, a "religionless Christianity" might evolve and what that would look like. Unfortunately, he was hanged by the Nazis before he could fully develop the idea.

He was clear, however, about what it would not look like: it would not be a Christianity that used the idea of God to fill the gaps in human understanding—neither the remaining puzzles about the universe nor a last resort to find strength in our failures. He thought a religionless Christianity would be "at the center of the village" rather than its boundaries: that is, in our strengths and goodness, as well as in our ignorance and alienation. He thought—hoped—that Christianity would not be a religion at all but rather somehow a presence in the real, secular world.

We will see that Bonhoeffer probably would have had some misgivings about more than one of our four paths. But of that, more later.

What Is a Religious Experience?

All the basic paths to Christian commitment we will be considering are based, not on speculative doctrines, but on people's experiences of the world and its disconnects—and of a possible way out. That is, they are based on "religious experiences." The unfortunate connotation of that term is that these experiences are always dramatic, sudden, and capable of "converting" us—that is, turning us around. The paradigmatic case is Paul's experience on the road to Damascus in which he, a leading and lethal persecutor of early Christians, is suddenly struck blind and has a vision of Jesus that changes his life. Needless to mention, most experiences of the world, its contradictions, and existential responses are not of this sort. More often, religious experiences involve a growing awareness of our situation and its resolution.

I have not had a large number of the more dramatic experiences, but I have had at least one, and I share it for whatever light, if any, it may shine on the phenomenon of religious experiences of the epiphany type. I was in a small town in rural Nicaragua in 1988, during the Contra War, with a small faith-based group called Witness for Peace that was there to bear witness to the interference by the US government in the popular, fledgling, revolutionary Sandinista movement. It was a Sunday, and since our immediate sponsors were the Roman Catholic group Pax Christi, we decided we would all go to mass. I had only a rudimentary understanding of the order of the mass, and I spoke almost no Spanish.

There was a reverence to the celebration, however, that was palpable and infectious. Sitting directly in front of me was a tiny, middle-aged Nicaraguan woman. When it came time to "pass the peace," she turned around and faced me. Instead of shaking hands, as Americans do in passing the peace, Nicaraguans gently take hold of your elbows, which leaves your hands on their elbows. It is a very tender gesture. Suddenly, as we looked into each other's eyes, the moment became strangely luminescent. I felt that we were together in some eternal moment, and my heart felt very full. I don't know if she felt anything similar, but it seemed to me then that she did.

This moment lasted perhaps three seconds, and it occurred nearly thirty-five years ago, but I can still see her face, and I feel I would recognize her if I saw her on the street. In any case, I will never forget the moment we shared.

Does such an experience "prove" anything about a religious dimension? Of course not. Do I think it "really" took place in another realm on—or beyond—the space-time continuum? That's a tougher question, depending on what you mean by "beyond," but my operating assumption is no. Does it sometimes give me entrée to another way of looking at the world? Yes.

It reminds me in some ways of the weird experience of the disciples that Christians call the Transfiguration:

Six days later, Jesus took with him Peter and James and his brother John and led them up a high mountain, by themselves. And he was transfigured before them, and his face shone like the sun, and his clothes became dazzling white. Suddenly there appeared to them Moses and Elijah, talking with him. Then Peter said to Jesus, "Lord, it is good for us to be here; if you wish, I will make three dwellings here, one for you, one for Moses, and one for Elijah." While he was still speaking, suddenly a bright cloud overshadowed them, and from the cloud a voice said, "This is my Son, the Beloved; with him I am well pleased; listen to him!" When the disciples heard this, they fell to the ground and were overcome by fear. But Jesus came and touched them, saying, "Get up and do not be afraid." And when they looked up, they saw no one except Jesus himself alone. (Matt 17:1–8 and parallels)

Peter is so undone that all he can think to offer is to build three "dwellings," of all things. What are we to make of this story? Is it supernatural? No, it's an extraordinary, psychedelic experience. Does it point to any particular content of the Christian message? No. Does it give us some insight into the extraordinary effect that the presence of Jesus had on the disciples? Yes.

While epiphanies of this sort, in which mysticism commingles with the ordinary world, are certainly of interest to students of religion, the more common religious experiences are on either one plane or the other. That is, they are either experiences of a felt, *personal* encounter with the divine, or they are mystical visions in which the ordinary world of things and persons melts away, and the person feels that he or she participates directly in the "ground of being," as Tillich says, nearly to the point of identification. *Tat tvam asi*, "That art thou," say the Hindu Upanishads.

Most, though not all, biblical descriptions of religious experiences are of the personal type, where the individual or group experiences a person-to-person encounter with God. These sorts of encounters are necessarily expressed in theistic language, properly understood as symbolic but often taken literally by Christians. In Scripture, God talks to individuals, strikes people dead, and so on, and if one feels personally connected to the divine, it is impossible to escape the use of this sort of theistic language. It is the only language we have for expressing personal encounters.

Mystical experience, on the other hand, is often described as ineffable, beyond the power of words to capture. "A mystic," as Ken Wilber says, "is not one who sees God as an object, but one who is immersed in God as an atmosphere."[5] Some Christian writers, from Meister Eckhardt to Jacob Böhme, write of a unitive experience with the divine. Others, like John of the Cross and Teresa of Avila, speak in the language of what has been called "spousal mysticism," the language of erotic union.

But neither personal encounter nor mystical participation is precisely faith, or at least not what Tillich calls "absolute faith." Neither type of experience, he says, is capable of prevailing over those moments of radical doubt and the incursion of radical meaninglessness and despair that many of us face eventually. Only the "courage to be" that springs from taking our anxiety and despair into ourselves and finding ourselves accepted and empowered in spite of it can constitute absolute faith. Accepted by whom? Empowered by whom? There is no theistic answer. At this point, we can say we have encountered the God who appears when the God of theism has disappeared; we have encountered the God above God.

WHAT DO WE MEAN BY *HOLY*?

In the year that King Uzziah died, I saw the Lord sitting on a throne, high and lofty; and the hem of his robe filled the temple. Seraphs were in attendance above him; each had six wings: with two they covered their faces, and with two they covered their feet, and with two they flew. And one called to another and said:

> "Holy, holy, holy is the Lord of hosts;
> the whole earth is full of his glory."

The pivots on the thresholds shook at the voices of those who called, and the house filled with smoke. And I said: "Woe is me! I am lost, for I am a man of unclean lips, and I live among a people of unclean lips; yet my eyes have seen the King, the Lord of hosts!"

Then one of the seraphs flew to me, holding a live coal that had been taken from the altar with a pair of tongs. The seraph touched my mouth with it and said: "Now that this has touched your lips, your guilt has departed and your sin is blotted out." Then I heard the voice of the Lord saying, "Whom shall I send, and who will go for us?" And I said, "Here am I; send me!" (Isa 6:1–8)

What just happened here? We don't know. We only know Isaiah's description of how it felt when he was called to be a prophet: the terrifying feeling of being overwhelmed, transported, found wanting, found unclean, and then feeling purified and weirdly confident. Rudolf Otto called it the *mysterium tremendum et fascinans*—the terrifying, yet somehow strangely intriguing, mystery of religious experience: "The daemonic-divine object may appear to the mind an object of horror and dread, but at the same time it is no less something that allures with a potent charm, and the creature, who trembles before it, utterly cowed and cast down, has always at the same time the impulse to turn to it, nay even to make it somehow his own."[6] It is the twofold experience of what Otto called "creature-feeling."

Now consider this:

[At the instant of the Big Bang,] particles burst into existence. From these particles will arise all the matter from which we and the universe around us are made. The matter and energy are so densely packed that 1 teaspoonful of this space weighs 100 million trillion trillion trillion pounds.[7]

[Ten billion years later,] a particularly remarkable molecule was formed by accident. We will call it the Replicator. . . . It had the extraordinary property of being able to create copies of itself. . . . The replicators that survived were the ones that built *survival machines* for themselves. . . . We are survival machines.[8]

Got "creature-feeling" yet? It is ironic that fundamentalist Christians insist on the Genesis story of creation as the "religious" version. The reason, of course, is that they are defending biblical inerrancy; for who could deny that the Big Bang and the theory of evolution pass the *mysterium tremendum* test? Fourteen billion years ago, most scientists think, the entire universe was concentrated in a single point with no dimensions. The point was not in space, because space did not yet exist. Suddenly this point began, for reasons yet unknown, to expand—infinitely. After one second it had become a ten-billion-degree soup of subatomic particles. Within three minutes, all the hydrogen atoms that will ever exist in the universe had been formed.

Skip ahead ten billion years. On one (as far as we know) of the estimated ten billion trillion (10,000,000, 000,000,000,000,000) planets produced by the Big Bang, the individual replicating gene has evolved; and, in Dawkins's formulation, it is this gene that becomes the unit of "survival of the fittest," or, more precisely, the survival of the stable. Some of the combinations that genes form are more stable than others, and they are the ones that survive. We human beings, like every other species of plant or animal, are a wildly fortuitous combination of genes that happen to be particularly stable. We are survival machines for genes. It's enough to make one "tremble before it, utterly cowed."

This is not to say that the awe inspired by contemplating our origin or the origin of the universe is necessarily religious awe. The scientist might very well be awed by the mysteries of the Big Bang and the probabilistic universe of quantum theory and the evolution of stable gene combinations called people, but he presumably would not identify his awe as a religious experience. (Interestingly, in *Living the Secular Life*, atheist Phil Zuckerman says that, at root, he is an "aweist.") Awe becomes religious only when we take it personally. It occurs when we look with the eye of the poet rather than the scientist, when we feel that there is a deep connection between the mysterious universe and our way of being-in-the-world. It is when we feel the power-of-being mirrored in our own souls. It is when, in our experience of the *mysterium tremendum*, we feel not only "cowed" but also "cast down," and not only overwhelmed but also humbled, having an impulse to "turn to it" and "make it our own."

The Gospels are full of stories of *mysterium tremendum*, the so-called signs or "mighty works" that Jesus is said to have performed during his ministry. What are we to make of them? In a world in which Schrödinger's famous cat is, according to some interpretations of quantum physics, either alive or dead, depending on its being observed, we can't rule out the possibility that some people may have had the key to changing our experience of reality. But let's not go there. This much we do know: the people who witnessed these events and/or passed the stories along as part of the oral tradition probably didn't look at them through the eyes of a scientist.

What Do We Really Know about the Historical Jesus? And What Does He Have to Do with Anything Anyway?

The first answer to the first question is—not much. We don't even know, for example, that he was a carpenter. Mark 6:3 seems to say he was, but the Greek word could also refer to another type of artisan. We don't even know whether Jesus was married, although we do know that it would have been odd in the extreme for a man of his age at that time not to be. (It would, of course, also be odd for the Gospels not to mention that he was married.)

The more negative descriptions of Jesus seem more reliable; for example, his family apparently thought he was crazy (Mark 3:21).

More importantly, the various "quests for the historical Jesus" have concluded that the gospel accounts, even those in Matthew, Mark, and Luke, are biased in favor of the beliefs the church had already adopted about the person and significance of Jesus: his status in relation to the divine, his Messiahship, the significance of his death and alleged resurrection, his ability to perform miracles, and so on.

A good summary of what we do and do not know about Jesus is provided by the Jewish scholar Geza Vermes in *The Real Jesus, Then and Now*. Vermes is a trustworthy guide with an unusual résumé. Born into a family of Jewish converts to Christianity, he attended the University of Louvain with the intention of becoming a Catholic priest. He eventually came to understand that he was not being called to either the priesthood or Christianity and pursued the education and career of a scholar, eventually ending up at Oxford. After the discovery of the Dead Sea Scrolls, he became a world expert on the subject and published a number of books. He has also written several books about Jesus and the New Testament. What is particularly useful about his work is not only his meticulous scholarship but the fact that he has no doctrinal ax to grind.

While we lack much biographical information about Jesus, says Vermes, the gospel accounts tell us a great deal about the effect he had on other people. He was clearly charismatic and attracted crowds wherever he went. His charisma apparently extended to healings and exorcisms.

Scholars are generally accepting of many of the so-called healing miracles, mainly because they are so central to the way the community remembered him—and to the way they connected his healings to his message—and because other charismatic Jewish figures at the time, like Hanina ben Dosa, were known as healers as well. (Hanina was also known as a rainmaker, so caution is advised.) Scholars generally refer to their healing acts as charismatic or psychosomatic healings. Current medical research on the so-called placebo effect and the medical significance of bedside manner lends some credibility to these labels. For example, studies have shown that patients are significantly more likely to get better if the practitioner touches them.

Incidentally, while the word *miracle* appears three times in the King James Version (1611) of the synoptic Gospels, the NRSV (1989) omits or corrects all three translations. It simply omits the reference in Mark 6:52, as does the original Greek text. In Mark 9:39, the NRSV translates the Greek word *dynamin* literally, as "deed[s] of power," and in Luke 23:8, it translates the Greek word *semeion* literally, as "sign." So much for the fundamentalist insistence on the miraculous nature of Jesus's "deeds of power."

In any event, Jesus's apparent charisma—the large crowds that followed him from place to place, the healings, the ascription to him of a unique relationship to God—is certainly a part of the picture that attracts and inspires many followers, then and now.

THE AMBIGUITY OF CHARISMA

Before we get too misty-eyed, however, we should consider the role that charisma has played in the enthusiastic acceptance of other figures in history. Some of the followers of former President Donald Trump hailed him from the outset as a semimessianic figure, chosen by God to restore the nation to its former glory. Former Press Secretary Sarah Huckabee Sanders was among those who claimed that it was God's will that Trump was elected. After he lost the 2020 election, many of those who stormed the Capitol conflated Trump with Jesus. Loud cheers erupted when the crowd was asked to demonstrate their belief in Jesus and Donald Trump.

At an even more demonic level, after Hitler's charismatic rise to power in the 1930s, many of the Protestant churches in Germany swore fidelity to the führer. One Protestant leader wrote, "Through his power, his honesty, his faith and his idealism . . . the Redeemer has found us [and] we know the Savior today has come!"[9] Resisters like Bonhoeffer and Martin Niemöller and the so-called Confessing Church were a minority.

Christopher Hitchens, one of the New Atheists, does a rather thorough job of laying out the outrages perpetrated in the name of religion, often by charismatic individuals. He catalogs the many instances of the world's religions having shown themselves to be violent, intolerant, racist, tribal, and bigoted, not to mention misogynistic and guilty of child abuse. That's not a difficult case to make, of course; nor is the claim that these outrages are often perpetrated by charismatic individuals. In recent history, we have witnessed the slaughter of Muslims at worship in mosques, suicide bombings of Christian communities in the Middle East, the mass shootings of Jews at worship in this country, and the ongoing brutal treatment of the Rohingya Muslims in Myanmar by—of all people—the Buddhists. Meanwhile, sex scandals involving priests and ministers continue to be uncovered, and patriarchy remains endemic in the church. Can religion "poison everything," as the subtitle of Hitchens's book claims? Alas, guilty as charged. But of course, you don't need to be an atheist to lament the rampant corruption of religion any more than you need to be an anarchist to lament the corruption of democracy.

Incidentally, the charismatic Jesus of the Gospels isn't responsible for the church's patriarchy and homophobia. Many of his closest disciples were women, and homosexuality and abortion are two subjects he has nothing whatsoever to say about in the Gospels. This is not to say that Hitchens is wrong that these are clear instances of how *religion* can "poison everything."

The Historical Jesus: Beyond the Charisma

In addition to the gospel portrayal of Jesus's charisma, it is his core message and, most importantly, the fact that he "wouldn't go away" after his death that are the most relevant parts of the gospel picture.

Many of Jesus's sayings—the ones that aren't influenced by the church's bias toward his Messiahship or sonship with God—are thought to be probably authentic, but they were handed down orally for many decades before any of the Gospels were written, so they may have been altered along the way. They are also very different from other sayings contained in the Gnostic gospels.

In general, however, as we have seen, Jesus saw his mission as prophetic: the proclamation of the kingdom of God and an attempt to bring repentant Jews into it. As Vermes points out, many parables run counter to the typical Christian understanding of the coming of the kingdom as a cataclysmic event slated to occur soon (although this theme is also discoverable in the Gospel accounts) and speak rather of a quiet, imperceptible change that is already happening: "He told them another parable: 'The kingdom of heaven is like yeast that a woman took and mixed in with three measures of flour until all it was leavened'" (Matt 13:33).

In other words, the kingdom is here now, quietly doing its work of penetrating and humanizing culture.

The most definitive passage is this: "Once Jesus was asked by the Pharisees when the kingdom of God was coming, and he answered, 'The kingdom of God is not coming with things that can be observed; nor will they say, "Look, here it is!" or "There it is!" For, in fact, the kingdom of God is among you'" (Luke 17:20–21).

Given the fact that no cataclysmic event has happened (yet, anyway), the picture of a kingdom within the current world would seem to speak more clearly to our time.

Jesus is portrayed as loving children and the *anawim*, the "little people," and judging those who were "puffed up," like the scribes and Pharisees.

In a nutshell, Jesus's preaching was centered on "God, the heavenly Father, the dignity of all human beings as children of God, a life turned into worship by total trust, an overwhelming sense of urgency to do one's duty without delaying tactics, a sanctification of the here and now, and, yes, the love of God through the love of one's neighbor."[10]

This is the picture formed by children brought up in the church, and it is a picture that adults who are still able to tune into the charisma are drawn to as well. It is a picture that still has the power to turn around the lives of alcoholics, drug addicts, and others who feel that something is wrong with them and are willing to face up to it. It is a picture that has brought about healing for many from a wide assortment of mental and spiritual disorders, as well as from existential anxiety and despair.

While the metaphysical status assigned to him in the Gospels does not help us understand his biography, it does reveal a great deal about Jesus and his acceptance by the people. The question is not "Was he 'really' the Messiah or the Son of God?" but rather "Why would people attribute those designations to a human being?" Again, it speaks to his charisma and the fact that he "spoke as one having authority." He was apparently, like Ramakrishna in nineteenth-century India, seen as a "God-intoxicated man," a man who was so totally absorbed in his relationship with God that he was considered transparent to the divine. And it also speaks to the fact that even after his crucifixion, his followers could not get him out of their minds and hearts; on the contrary, they found themselves able to heal and persuade others as Jesus had.

Scholars generally think it is highly unlikely that Jesus referred to himself as the "Son of God," and in any event, that term, as used in the Synoptics, seems to be a synonym for "Messiah" rather than "the second person of the Trinity." The title of "Messiah" (in Greek,

Christos, or Christ) is itself problematic, as the Jewish understanding of the Messiah as a political figure in the line of David does not fit at all with the life of Jesus. *Messiah* literally indicates "anointed one," so it is at least possible that Jesus considered himself anointed to do God's work. It seems more likely to scholars, though, that the community, in trying to make sense of his ministry, applied the term to him.

So what of Jesus's death? Did he "die for our sins?" Vermes thinks he merely "did the wrong thing at the wrong place and the wrong time." He caused an uproar at the Temple by driving out the money changers during Passover, a time when the Roman authorities were particularly nervous about rebellion because of the large number of pilgrims in Jerusalem.

The resurrection, says Vermes, was the disciples' experience "in their hearts" that Jesus had risen from the dead, a vision that empowered them to do charismatic acts like his. Interestingly, some of the Gnostic gospels also attribute the resurrection appearances to mystical visions rather than encounters in the flesh. As Tillich used to tell his classes, don't ask what the *New York Times* photographer would have captured on Easter morning. It's irrelevant. If Christ is alive for you now, it doesn't matter. And if he isn't, it doesn't matter either.

Is the Language of Existentialism Passé?

Søren Kierkegaard died in 1855; Paul Tillich in 1965. Is their religious language still relevant today?

More than two-thirds of the US population was not yet born when Tillich died. Tillich told us that each generation must reinterpret the Christian message for its own historical moment. Is the language of existentialism, the language of subjective human experience, still relevant to our moment? As one who lived in Tillich's moment, I really can't tell. If you are one of the two-thirds who make up the post-1965 generation(s), you probably can.

5

GOD IS GOOD?

"You might as well pray to Peter Rabbit," says Spike to his girlfriend, Hilary, whom he has just "caught" saying her prayers.

"Explain consciousness," counters Hilary, incongruously. This conversation has clearly been going on over several days or weeks.

"When did your mind turn into a party balloon?" asks Spike, ignoring her demand to explain consciousness. Spike is confident that all human behavior, including consciousness, has been determined by natural selection: "evo-bio," evolutionary biology.

Spike: The Good Samaritan? Evo-bio. Culture, empathy, faith, hope, and charity, all the flip sides of egoism, come back to biology, because there just ain't anywhere else to come from except three pounds of gray matter wired up in your head like a map of the

> London Underground with eighty-six billion sta-
> tions connected thirty trillion ways. . . .[1]

So begins Tom Stoppard's hilarious and supersmart play *The Hard Problem*. The hard problem is the mind-body problem: What is consciousness? Is it just a by-product of brain activity? Do we have independent minds capable of creating and directing thought?

Exactly what this question has to do with the question of God, neither Stoppard nor any of his characters explain, other than to imply that both seem to challenge the biological model of evolutionary determinism. (Interestingly, according to Vedanta texts, God can be described as *sat-chit-ananda*, Sanskrit for "being-*consciousness*-bliss.") In any event, Spike maintains that all human behavior has been selected for because it was advantageous to the survival of the species. No need for "mind," no need for God.

Spike's position isn't merely theoretical. Many people who have gotten high on cannabis, including me, can testify to the experience of going from normal consciousness ("I think this, I think that") to the perception that the brain (?) has already had that thought just a nanosecond ago, and the mind is merely running along behind, trying to catch up and "own" the thought.

Fun stuff, but the argument takes an even more interesting twist when Hilary confronts Spike with the notion of altruism, good for its own sake. Motherly love, insists Hilary, is a *virtue*. Its only "virtue," says Spike, consists in its *utility*—in maximizing the survival of the mother's genes.

Exactly what the question of good has to do with the question of God isn't clear either, but both characters tacitly accept that there's a connection.

Iris Murdoch's essay "On God and Good" explores the same territory.

Murdoch was one of several well-known women philosophers at Oxford in the mid-twentieth century. She made her mark as a novelist as well, winning the prestigious Booker Prize for her 1978 novel, *The Sea, the Sea*. She is probably best known to general audiences for her extraordinary number of love affairs with both men and women (A. N. Wilson described her as "one of those delightful young women . . . who was prepared to go to bed with almost anyone") and for her tragic descent into Alzheimer's, which was documented by her husband, English literary critic and novelist John Bayley, whose memoir was adapted for the movie *Iris* in 2001.

Murdoch saw the connection between the ideas of good and God—as well as art—in the fact that all three of them depend, not on metaphysical belief, but on a refocusing of *attention*, a notion she borrowed from the well-known, mystical, political thinker and philosopher Simone Weil. In her best-known parable, Murdoch imagines a mother-in-law, M, who feels superior and judgmental toward her daughter-in-law, D. M considers D's behavior "common," but she acts graciously toward D and shows no sign of the contempt she feels. At the same time, M realizes that her feelings are base and may be caused by jealousy, so she sets out to change her view of D, trying to make it more truthful, less selfish. Instead of "common," she will say "fresh and naïve." This is not a mere verbal trick: M is training herself to *see* D in a more just, truthful, and unselfish way.

Compassion, Murdoch is saying, is simply realism. It is seeing and paying attention to the truth that others have the same claim on our consideration that we ourselves have. What motivates our attempt to see the world as it really is, is love. The role of inner life and "inner work" in morality, religion, and art, says Murdoch, is to seek out another source of energy—an image of God or a realistic reappraisal of our view of other people—that will reorient the way we naturally, and self-centeredly, see the world.

My friend Bob Lohbauer, who embraces no religion, recently shared with me the following story, which profoundly illustrates the way in which truly seeing another person can transform the way we behave toward them and sometimes transform the other person's behavior as well.

One morning during the first week of March 2017, my wife and I were vacationing in New Orleans, the French Quarter to be exact. It was sometime around 10:00 a.m. We were wandering up Royale Street, looking for a place that served breakfast. As we approached Canal Street, we saw a white man ranting at no one in particular. But he was loud, angry, and obscene. Because he had planted himself in the center of the sidewalk, my wife went around to the left of him and I to the right. When we were about halfway by him, he grabbed my wife by the arm. I had been watching him carefully, so of course I reacted. I grabbed his right arm, spun him to me, and said "Get your hands off her." And I drew back my fist. He did the same. We looked at each other. And as if a switch had been thrown, I looked into his eyes and saw his pain, his humanity. I heard myself saying "You know you don't have to do this." Immediately his eyes softened as I'm sure had mine and he accepted my proffered hand. He then immediately stormed toward Canal Street screaming at a group of Hispanics on the corner to "get out of my country and go back where you came from."

Murdoch herself shows no evidence of a religious worldview, but she knows the territory. What the three modes of thought—morality, religion, and art—have in common is *transcendence*, rising above our own egoism. (Anne Lamott says another word for God is "not me.") Murdoch quotes Paul's letter to the Philippians on refocusing our attention: "Whatsoever things are true, whatsoever things are honest, whatsoever things are just, whatsoever things are pure, whatsoever things are lovely, whatsoever things are of good report; if there be any virtue, and if there be any praise, think on these things" (Phil 4:8, KJV).

What is the relevance of these thoughts of Tom Stoppard and Iris Murdoch to our project? All four of the paths into a Christian worldview and a Christian life that we will be looking at—the kingdom of God, the Holy Spirit, the experience of forgiveness, and Christ in you—involve a different *vision*, a different way of *seeing* the world and other people.

Tom Stoppard's play acknowledges that consciousness, altruism, and religiosity are indeed a "hard problem," one that can be "solved" objectively by theories of evolutionary biology but are experienced subjectively as mysteries of the human spirit. One can argue, as Spike does, that consciousness and free will are simply brain blips. But can I really say that about *my* consciousness, *my* free will? Stoppard's Hilary would say no, as would the existentialists.

For Iris Murdoch morality, religiosity, and art all spring from this shift in point of view, as we see the world in an un-self-centered way and seek out "another source of energy" to help us live out our vision.

The remaining chapters will try to show that there are several paths to a Christian experience and a Christian life that are built on such profound changes in point of view. These paths are not objectively provable, nor are they able to be adequately summarized in beliefs and rules. They are "religionless," the result of religious experience, yet they point the way to life in the world. They illustrate the paradox that while objectively there is no provable God, experientially, Mary is his mother.

6

ENVISIONING A KINGDOM OF GOD

The entire narrative in the first three Gospels is explicitly centered on Jesus's preaching of the coming kingdom. If a Christian says that their faith has been inspired by the picture of Jesus and his message presented in the synoptic Gospels, we can safely assume that their vision of the kingdom of God is central to their faith.

So the first path into Christian life and worldview we will look at is Jesus's picture of the kingdom of God.

Mark's Gospel, the earliest of the three and a major source for both Matthew and Luke, begins with Jesus launching his ministry by announcing this "good news of God": "The time is fulfilled, and the kingdom of God has come near; repent, and believe in the good news" (Mark 1:15 and parallel, Matt 4:17). (David Bentley Hart's translation: "*change your hearts* and believe in the good news.")

Mark has no birth story, no shepherds, no mangers, no wise men. His Gospel begins with Jesus's ministry, following his baptism by John the Baptist and his temptations in the wilderness.

That ministry was centered on proclaiming to Israel the coming of the kingdom of God (usually, but not always, rendered by Matthew as "kingdom of heaven"), and the passages in the synoptic Gospels that report this proclamation address our questions about the kingdom.

WHEN WILL THE KINGDOM COME?

This question does not have an easy answer. A parable unique to Matthew points to the future, to the "end of the age." Hart translates it, "the consummation of the age." This is not about the calendar; this is eschatological talk—that is to say, talk about the "end time," the final step in God's plan for salvation:

> The kingdom of heaven may be compared to someone who sowed good seed in his field; but while everybody was asleep, an enemy came and sowed weeds among the wheat, and then went away. So when the plants came up and bore grain, then the weeds appeared as well. And the slaves of the householder came and said to him, "Master, did you not sow good seed in your field? Where, then, did these weeds come from?" He answered, "An enemy has done this." The slaves said to him, "Then do you want

us to go and gather them?" But he replied, "No; for in gathering the weeds you would uproot the wheat along with them. Let both of them grow together until the harvest; and at harvest time I will tell the reapers, Collect the weeds first and bind them in bundles to be burned, but gather the wheat into my barn." (Matt 13:24b–30)

When asked by the disciples to explain the parable, Jesus says that the harvest is the "end of the age" and that the Son of Man (perhaps a reference, not to Jesus himself, but to the apocalyptic Old Testament figure in Daniel 7) will send his angels to separate the evildoers from the righteous, throwing the evildoers into the furnace of fire and causing the righteous to "shine like the sun in the kingdom of their Father" (Matt 13:43).

Is it Jesus's literal belief that the appearance of the kingdom of God will occur at some future point "at the end of the age?" We are in "eschatological time" here and categories like past/present/future may not make a great deal of sense when applied to an imagined time beyond time. In any event, Matthew's parable does seem to place the inbreaking of the kingdom in the future, albeit an "eschatological future" beyond all futures.

A passage from Mark is seemingly more specific in placing the inbreaking of the kingdom in the "real" future: "And he said to them, 'Truly I tell you, there are some standing here who will not taste death until they

see that the kingdom of God has come with power'"
(Mark 9:1 and parallels).

Then there are the passages that say that the kingdom of God is "among us" now or "in our midst" or
possibly "within us." Matthew attributes the following
parables to Jesus:

> He put before them another parable: "The kingdom of
> heaven is like a mustard seed that someone took and
> sowed in his field; it is the smallest of all the seeds, but
> when it has grown it is the greatest of shrubs and becomes
> a tree, so that the birds of the air come and make nests in
> its branches." (Matt 13:31–32)

> The kingdom of heaven is like treasure hidden in a field,
> which someone found and hid; then in his joy he goes
> and sells all that he has and buys that field. (Matt 13:44)

These certainly don't seem to point to an apocalyptic event in the future but rather to an event that is happening now and, in the second parable, an event that
can happen *for us* now.

In a passage unique to Luke, Jesus says, "Once
Jesus was asked by the Pharisees when the kingdom of
God was coming, and he answered, 'The kingdom
of God is not coming with things that can be observed;
nor will they say, "Look, here it is!" or "There it is!"

For, in fact, the kingdom of God is among you'" (Luke 17:20–21).

The King James Version had translated the passage as "the kingdom of God is *within* you," but most modern translators felt that this mystical rendering was unlikely. Surprisingly, Hart disagrees and makes the case, based on Luke's other uses of *within* and *among*, that the passage probably means "within."

In either case, the kingdom of God is not coming in some vague future but is here and now. In some passages, Jesus's casting out of demons is itself a sign of the inbreaking of the kingdom: "You say that I cast out the demons by Beelzebul. . . . But if it is by the finger of God that I cast out the demons, then the kingdom of God has come to you" (Luke 11:18b, 20 and parallels).

Are these several passages contradictory? Or does Jesus sometimes envision the eschatological kingdom of God as being in the future and at other times already present, if we but had eyes to see?

Whatever the answer to that question may be, a sophisticated, modern Christian whose entrée to Christianity is Jesus's vision of the kingdom likely experiences it as being among us or within us, if for no other reason than the fact that an apocalyptic event hasn't happened in the time frame Jesus apparently predicted. In fact, the church was initially embarrassed that years, and then centuries, went by without the anticipated apocalypse.

When Geza Vermes writes of Jesus's "sanctification of the here and now," he is probably thinking in part of the picture Jesus paints of the kingdom among us.

So one important component of an inspirational vision of the kingdom of God is that it is here and now and that it can be entered by those who are willing to "sell all that they have" to buy the field that contains that hidden treasure.

Note that even the kingdom-in-the-future version is not basically about believing a pseudoscientific prediction of a future catastrophe in the same vein as, say, a scientific prediction of future global warming. It is rather about a vision of the ultimate purpose and value of our lives.

As we will see, many people inspired by the vision of the kingdom of God also experience it as a picture of how society should work, and not simply as an ethic for individual behavior. Jesus himself does not seem to have had a particular program in mind for the reform of society, but this may be because Judea and Galilee were under total domination by Rome, and a social agenda—at least a peaceful one—would have been irrelevant.

In either case, the kingdom of God is clearly a vision that can be shared by the "religionless" of Bonhoeffer's prophecy.

WHO IS THE KINGDOM FOR?

In the synoptic Gospels, Jesus gives several answers to the question of who will be received into the kingdom. We have already seen—in Mark's rendition of Jesus's announcement of his ministry—that all who are willing to "turn" (repent, change their hearts) are welcome to enter the kingdom. This is, in fact, the "good news," or gospel.

Moreover, Jesus says, it is never too late to turn. Those who enter at the eleventh hour are as welcome as those who entered early, even though Jesus admits that by human standards, that is patently unfair:

> For the kingdom of heaven is like a landowner who went out early in the morning to hire laborers for his vineyard. After agreeing with the laborers for the usual daily wage, he sent them into his vineyard. When he went out about nine o'clock, he saw others standing idle in the marketplace; and he said to them, "You also go into the vineyard, and I will pay you whatever is right." So they went. When he went out again about noon and about three o'clock, he did the same. And about five o'clock he went out and found others standing around; and he said to them, "Why are you standing here idle all day?" They said to him, "Because no one has hired us." He said to them, "You also go into the vineyard." When evening came, the owner of the vineyard said to his manager, "Call the laborers and give them

their pay, beginning with the last and then going to the first." When those hired about five o'clock came, each of them received the usual daily wage. Now when the first came, they thought they would receive more; but each of them also received the usual daily wage. And when they received it, they grumbled against the landowner, saying, "These last worked only one hour, and you have made them equal to us who have borne the burden of the day and the scorching heat." But he replied to one of them, "Friend, I am doing you no wrong; did you not agree with me for the usual daily wage? Take what belongs to you and go; I choose to give to this last the same as I give to you. Am I not allowed to do what I choose with what belongs to me? Or are you envious because I am generous?" So the last will be first, and the first will be last. (Matt 20:1–16)

This is what Christians call "grace," or gift. Acceptance into the kingdom is available to all who "change their hearts."

Grace is also available regardless of social status. In the parable of the feast, Jesus tells the story of a man who invited several guests to dinner, but when he sent his slave out to tell the guests that everything was ready, they had various excuses for not coming: one felt he needed to go see the new piece of land he had bought, another was about to try out five new yoke of oxen, another said he had just gotten married. When the slave reported all this to his master, the master was furious. He said to his slave, "Go out at once into the streets and lanes of the town and bring in the poor, the crippled, the blind, and the lame. . . . For I tell you, none of those who were invited will taste my dinner" (Luke 14:21b, 24; parallel in Matt 22:1–10).

Passages such as this inspired the "social gospel" movement at the turn of the twentieth century. Under the leadership of Walter Rauschenbusch and others, this group of theologians and clergy emphasized that the kingdom of God is a blueprint for radical social change and not simply a spiritual destination for individuals. The most explicit passage underlying the social gospel is at the end of Matthew's chapter 25, where Jesus prophesies that the "Son of Man" at the close of the age will say,

> "I was hungry and you gave me food, I was thirsty and you gave me something to drink, I was a stranger and you welcomed me, I was naked and you gave me cloth-ing, I was sick and you took care of me, I was in prison and you visited me." Then the righteous will answer [the Son of Man], "Lord, when was it that we saw you hungry and gave you food, or thirsty and gave you something to drink? And when was it that we saw you a stranger and welcomed you, or naked and gave you clothing? And when was it that we saw you sick or in prison and visited you?" [The Son of Man will answer,] "Truly I tell you, just as

you did it to one of the least of these who are members of
my family, you did it to me." (Matt 25:35–40)

Even if Jesus himself did not intend these passages
as a social blueprint, theologians like Rauschenbusch
felt that they lent themselves to that interpretation.

The social gospel movement was influential in passing labor laws and creating the settlement movement,
and its influence has lived on in the movements for civil
rights, women's rights, gay, transsexual, and gender
nonconforming rights, and liberation theology strug-
gles, as well as in the sanctuary movement.

The Southern Christian Leadership Conference,
under the leadership of Rev. Dr. Martin Luther King Jr.
and Rev. Ralph Abernathy, was a revolutionary social
force, and many clergy and laypeople, Black and white,
joined the movement out of Christian conviction.
Nonetheless, in 1963, James Baldwin wrote in *The Fire
Next Time* that white Christian churches had been a
major contributor to incipient racism.

Still, even some white evangelicals, not generally
involved in liberal social movements, became activists,
and Jim Wallis's Sojourners community attracted con-
siderable support. As the more socially activist mainline
denominations lost members and influence in recent
decades, mainline seminaries, such as Union in New
York City, nonetheless placed greater and greater stress

on social justice for nonwhite people, women, and people identifying as LGBTQ.

Yet sadly, not enough has happened to change James Baldwin's 1963 indictment of the Christian churches' contribution to racism. A recent book by Robert P. Jones of the Public Opinion Research Institute reports that recent polls demonstrate that "the more racist attitudes a person holds, the more likely he or she is to identify as a white Christian." In fact, "If you were recruiting for a white supremacist cause on a Sunday morning, you'd likely have more success hanging out in the parking lot of an average white Christian church—evangelical Protestant, mainline Protestant, or Catholic—than approaching whites sitting out services at the local coffee shop."[1]

Jesus had stressed that we can't simply accept the gift of grace and carry on as usual. In the parable of the talents (a unit of money), Jesus tells the story of a man who went on a journey and entrusted his money to his slaves. Most of them used their share to earn some additional money, but one of them said he knew the master was a harsh man, so he hid the talent that had been entrusted to him in the ground. The master berates him for not having grown what he was given (Matt 25:14–30 and Luke 19:12–27).

Even though the invitation to grace is available to all, only certain people are likely to accept the invitation. In the so-called Beatitudes at the beginning of Matthew's rendering of the Sermon on the Mount, Jesus says that the "poor in spirit," whom Hart calls "the destitute, abject in spirit," will be blessed to enter the kingdom of heaven (Matt 5:3). Luke simply calls them "the poor." After centuries of taking a back seat to Matthew's "poor in spirit," Luke may have been on the right track after all, as one group that Jesus does not see as candidates for the kingdom is the rich. Jesus tells a rich man that if he wants to make a total commitment, he should sell all he has, give the money to the poor, and follow Jesus. Then Jesus tells him, he will have treasure in heaven. The rich man goes away shocked and grieved, "for he had many possessions." Then Jesus says to the disciples, "'How hard it will be for those who have wealth to enter the kingdom of God!' And the disciples were perplexed at these words. But Jesus said to them again, 'Children, how hard it is to enter the kingdom of God! It is easier for a camel to go through the eye of a needle than for someone who is rich to enter the kingdom of God'" (Mark 10:23b–25 and parallels).

The disciples are astounded and ask him, "Then who can be saved?" Jesus doesn't directly answer their question, but in all three of the synoptic Gospels, this story is immediately preceded by a scene in which people bring children to Jesus to have him touch them. The disciples speak sternly to the parents, but Jesus indignantly tells them, "Let the little children come to me; do not stop them; for it is to such as these that the kingdom of

God belongs. Truly I tell you, whoever does not receive the kingdom of God as a little child will never enter it" (Mark 10:14b–15 and parallels).

The issue for the rich—and presumably, for most adults—is that we have given priority to something other than the kingdom. We have ascribed ultimacy to something other than what is truly ultimate, the kingdom of God. We have committed idolatry.

Of our four paths, the kingdom of God is probably the one most in sync with Bonhoeffer's vision of a "religionless Christianity."

The kingdom of God is the vision underlying Martin Luther King's "religionless" notion of the Beloved Community, a society based on love but, equally importantly, on justice.

As Dr. King put it, "Power without love is reckless and abusive, and love without power is sentimental and anemic. Power at its best is love implementing the demands of justice, and justice at its best is power correcting everything that stands against love."[2] Both King's and Bonhoeffer's visions are of a kingdom-of-God-in-the-world that demands not fine sentiments or religious separation from the world but something far more difficult: fair and equal treatment of men and women of all races and ethnicities, all variations of gender identification and sexual preference, all religious affiliations or lack thereof. The demand is without exception and imposes itself on us not only as individuals but also as a society. It is too easy, as Dr. King knew, for Americans to be glib about these principles. The Black Lives Matter movement has reminded us yet again that we are far from the Beloved Community or the kingdom of God.

Bonhoeffer's "religionless Christianity," like Dr. King's Beloved Community, is a further development of Jesus's kingdom vision, a faith that lives in the messy midst of a secular world without false attempts to "transcend" the world through metaphysics or inwardness or an otherworldly vision of the church. It is too late, Bonhoeffer says, for such moves in a "world come of age." The only genuine transcendence left is participation in the being of Jesus in his "existence for others." The way in which Jesus transcends the world is not by being "the second person of the Trinity" but by being the man for others.

If this "participation" in Jesus's "being" sounds like a picture of individual piety in an otherwise religionless world, it is clear that this is not at all what Bonhoeffer had in mind. It is too late, he says, not only for metaphysics and creeds, but also for individual piety and inwardness. These are retreats from the world; Christianity must somehow live fully in the secular world.

Yet as Jesus makes clear, the kingdom of God, or the Beloved Community, is not just another social or political ideology. We must "receive" the kingdom as a child, rather than simply think it up.

From a worldly perspective, though (leaving aside the individual's "participation in Jesus"), it is unclear exactly what religionless Christianity would look like, how it would differ from just plain religionlessness. Bonhoeffer asks himself, "What do a church, a community, a sermon, a liturgy, a Christian life mean in a religionless world?"[3] It is a pity that Bonhoeffer was not granted enough time to think through or live out his vision of the kingdom of God in a religionless world. Perhaps King's Beloved Community is as close as we can get to uncovering what a "religionless Christianity" would be.

True stories of actual people and ordinary situations, however, sometimes show us how it's done. Phillip Hoose's book *Hoosiers* tells the story of the 1961 desegregation of the basketball court in Meadowood Park in all-white Speedway, Indiana. It was the year the blond-haired Van Arsdale twins, Tom and Dick, graduated from their high school on the other side of Indianapolis, and in basketball-crazed Indiana, they were royalty. They were to go on to star in college and the NBA, but in 1961, they had just gotten their driver's licenses and could get around greater Indianapolis.

Meadowood Park was also legendary. Games of pickup basketball happened there every evening and bred several future college and NBA stars, all white. One night a caravan of cars arrived from out of town with "the Vans" in the lead car. Behind them was a line of cars filled with black players from Indianapolis. The Vans asked if they could play some ball, and of course, the awestruck Speedway players said yes. They played until dark. The next night they were back, the caravan again led by the twins. The following night the same thing happened. Then one night the caravan arrived without the Vans; and the Vans never came back.

Not a moralistic word had been spoken. Not a word of any kind had been spoken. The Van Arsdale twins just knew they had power, and they used it for justice. It was an example of Dr. King's dictum that "power at its best is love implementing the demands of justice, and justice at its best is power correcting everything that stands against love."

But is the demand to put the kingdom of God and existence-for-others above our own interests unrealistic? Is it even undesirable, as Nietzsche thought? These are among the questions posed by "religionless Christianity" and the vision of the kingdom of God. In the end, the religious and the nonreligious alike must choose what is ultimate for us, as individuals and as a society. That "choice" may be tacit, or passive, or even unconscious, but it is an existential "choice" nonetheless. It is manifest in the way we live our lives and order our common life.

Jesus himself lives out the kingdom of God by treating women, adulterers, the poor and marginalized—the "tax-collectors and sinners," as his detractors characterize his friends—with total dignity as children of God and preferring their company to that of the pompous, the hypocritical, and the rich. (Interestingly, Bonhoeffer writes to Bethge, "I often ask myself why a 'Christian instinct' often draws me more to the religionless people than to the religious.")[4]

A key element of Jesus's vision of the kingdom is forgiveness. In Matthew's Gospel, Peter asks how often he should forgive. As many as seven times? Jesus replies, "Not seven times, but seventy-seven times" (Matt 18:22 in NRSV; other translations say, "seventy times seven"). In any case, Jesus clearly doesn't mean either 77 or 490; rather, we should always forgive, just as we have been forgiven.

He tells a parable about a king who sets out to settle accounts with his slaves. One owes a great deal of money and is unable to pay, so the king orders him, his wife and children, and all his possessions to be sold to pay the debt. The slave begs for patience, and the king takes pity on him and forgives the entire debt. The slave then comes upon a fellow slave who owes him money, grabs him by the throat, and demands that he pay up. When his fellow slave is unable to pay and begs for patience, he has him thrown into prison. The other slaves report this to the king, who then summons the slave and says to him, "'You wicked slave! I forgave you all that debt because you pleaded with me. Should you not have had mercy on your fellow slave, as I had mercy on you?' And in anger his lord handed him over to be tortured until he should pay his entire debt. So my heavenly Father will also do to every one of you, if you do not forgive your brother or sister from your heart" (Matt 18:32b–35).

This violent metaphor clashes rather harshly with the popular image of "gentle Jesus, meek and mild," but it makes the point. The demand for forgiveness is a deadly serious part of accepting entry into the kingdom. As Jesus says in the Lord's prayer, "Forgive us our debts, as we also have forgiven our debtors" (Matt 6:9–13). In case we missed the point, Matthew has Jesus spell it out for us: "For if you forgive others their trespasses, your heavenly Father will also forgive you; but if you do not forgive others, neither will your Father forgive your trespasses" (Matt 6:14–15).

The Lord's prayer is a prayer explicitly about the kingdom of God: "Your kingdom come, your will be done, on earth as it is in heaven."

Central to Jesus's vision of that kingdom is, of course, the demand to love God and our neighbor. Sayings from the first three Gospels about this demand to love God and neighbor round out Jesus's vision of the kingdom and its citizenship requirements:

> One of the scribes came near and heard them disputing with one another, and seeing that he answered them well,

he asked him, "Which commandment is the first of all?" Jesus answered, "The first is, 'Hear, O Israel: the Lord our God, the Lord is one; you shall love the Lord your God with all your heart, and with all your soul, and with all your mind, and with all your strength.' The second is this, 'You shall love your neighbor as yourself.' There is no other commandment greater than these." Then the scribe said to him, "You are right, Teacher; you have truly said that 'he is one, and besides him there is no other'; and 'to love him with all the heart, and with all the understanding, and with all the strength,' and 'to love one's neighbor as oneself,'—this is much more important than all whole burnt offerings and sacrifices." When Jesus saw that he answered wisely, he said to him, "You are not far from the kingdom of God." (Mark 12:28–34 and parallels)

The popular conception of this passage is that the demand to love one's neighbor is Jesus's extension of the Old Testament law. Actually, Jesus, always the Jew, is paraphrasing a passage from the Torah: Leviticus 19:18.

But what could it possibly mean to *command* someone to love their neighbor as themself? How can anyone make themself love somebody they don't love? It's clearly not possible if you think of love as a feeling or an attraction or a bond of friendship. Kierkegaard says the command is at bottom a requirement to recognize that you and your neighbor have equality before God. It is a matter of adopting a different way of looking, a refocusing of *attention*, as Iris Murdoch and Simone Weil have said. In Santayana's language, the revelation of the fact that we and our neighbor are "equal before God" opens new vistas and reveals "another world to live in." That world is what Jesus calls the kingdom of God.

The Urgency and Ultimacy of the Kingdom

You will remember that, according to Geza Vermes, one theme of the synoptic narratives is "the overwhelming sense of urgency to do one's duty without delaying tactics." In the parable of the bridesmaids, Jesus compares the kingdom of heaven to ten bridesmaids who took their lamps and went to meet the bridegroom. Five of them took no extra oil with them. The bridegroom was delayed, and when he was about to appear, they all ran to trim their lamps, and the "foolish" five saw that their lamps were going out. They asked the "wise" five to share their oil and the "wise" replied that there was not enough oil for all, and they had better go to the dealers to buy some. While they were gone, the bridegroom appeared, and the entire wedding party went into the banquet and shut the door. When the foolish five returned and asked the bridegroom to open the door, he replied, "Truly I tell you, I don't know you." Jesus concludes, "Keep awake therefore, for you know neither the day nor the hour" (Matt 25:12–13).

Clearly, this is an instance of Jesus placing the kingdom in the future, but in the sense of "at any moment." It is also an instance that shows the urgency Jesus places on our decision to "turn," "change our hearts," and enter the kingdom of heaven.

More importantly, several of Jesus's words about the kingdom of God reveal that Jesus felt that the decision to "turn," to accept acceptance into the kingdom of God, was the ultimate decision facing humanity. Recall Tillich's definition of faith as "ultimate concern," and consider the following passages.

In his conversation with the man who had many possessions, we have already seen Jesus call out the fact that the man has assigned the ultimate place in his life to his wealth rather than to the kingdom: "Jesus, looking at him, loved him and said, 'You lack one thing; go, sell what you own, and give the money to the poor, and you will have treasure in heaven; then come, follow me'" (Mark 10:21 and parallels).

The man is unable to comply.

To another he said, "Follow me." But he said, "Lord, first let me go and bury my father" [that is, look after his father till he died]. But Jesus said to him, "Let the dead bury their own dead; but as for you, go and proclaim the kingdom of God." Another said, "I will follow you, Lord; but let me first say farewell to those at my home." Jesus said to him, "No one who puts a hand to the plow and looks back is fit for the kingdom of God." (Luke 9:59–62 and parallel in Matt 8:21–22)

These rather harsh, even brutal, passages underscore both the urgency and the ultimacy of Jesus's demand for a radical decision to enter the kingdom.

In two parables unique to Matthew, the pearl of great price and the treasure in the field (Matt 13:44–45), Jesus tells of people who sold all they had to buy the pearl and the field.

The starkly radical character of this decision is reflected in the spiritual narratives of other cultures as well. For example, in the Cherokee fable "The Fight of Two Wolves within You":

An old Cherokee is teaching his grandson about life:

"A fight is going on inside me," he said to the boy.

"It is a terrible fight and it is between two wolves. One is evil—he is anger, envy, sorrow, regret, greed, arrogance, self-pity, guilt, resentment, inferiority, lies, false pride, superiority, and ego."

He continued, "The other is good—he is joy, peace, love, hope, serenity, humility, kindness, benevolence, empathy, generosity, truth, compassion, and faith. The same fight is going on inside you—and inside every other person too."

The grandson thought about it for a minute and then asked his grandfather: "Which wolf will win?"

The old Cherokee simply replied, "The one you feed."[5]

The Covenant Renewal Service of the United Methodist Church expresses the radical ultimacy of Jesus's demand in these stark terms:

> *I am no longer my own, but yours.*
> *Put me to what you will, rank me with whom you will;*
> *put me to doing, put me to suffering;*
> *let me be employed for you, or laid aside for you,*
> *exalted for you, or brought low for you;*
> *let me be full,*
> *let me be empty, let me have all things,*
> *let me have nothing:*
> *I freely and wholeheartedly yield all things*
> *to your pleasure and disposal.*[6]

The kingdom of God is a radical *vision*, a different way of seeing, if you will, inspiring a different way of being-in-the-world. But it is more than just Iris Murdoch's observation that the lives of others have the same claim on us that our own lives do. If that were our entire revelation, we wouldn't be very successful in acting on it. We must also, as Tillich says, be "grasped" by the power of the kingdom of God. Without Jesus's crucifixion and the subsequent strange experiences of the disciples that Jesus was not done with them yet, the kingdom of God vision would have remained just that: a vision. It would have lacked the power to transform lives.

The kingdom may be envisioned either as coming "at the end of the age," which is already on the immediate horizon, or as being "in our midst," or even within us. In any event, the time for decision is now. It is available to all who "turn," provided they are able to accept such an unmerited gift. It is never too late to turn and accept this gift. It is available to the "poor in spirit" and to those who accept it in a childlike spirit. It is not available to those who place something else above it in importance. It requires further action from us: complete forgiveness of our fellow human beings, wholehearted love of God and his kingdom, and love of our neighbors as ourselves.

This path does not require any metaphysical or doctrinal beliefs. Even the word *God* is mainly useful as it underlies this vision of the *kingdom* of God. The name of God is the indicator of the ultimacy of the kingdom vision and an expression of the *power* to realize the vision in the here and now.

7

HOW HOLY IS THE HOLY SPIRIT?

Living the kingdom of God may be the path closest to Bonhoeffer's "religionless Christianity," but our remaining three paths—seeking the guidance of the Holy Spirit, accepting the grace of forgiveness, and opening ourselves to the Christ within us—are all vulnerable to his criticisms of individualistic alternatives to living fully in the world. If these paths were ends in themselves, if any of them were used to avoid full participation in the secular world, this criticism would be inescapable and damning. But like all paths, they lead somewhere; they have a destination. And in keeping with Bonhoeffer's vision of Christianity, their destination is full participation in the secular world and its transformation into the kingdom of God.

So the second Christian path we will look at is the personal relationship with what Christians call the Holy Spirit.

Not only does one's relationship with the Spirit not rely on doctrine, but the creed writers had difficulty even *making* it into doctrine. After several dramatic statements about the Son, the best the bishops at Nicaea could come up with for the Spirit was "the giver of life, who proceeds from the Father and the Son, and who with the Father and the Son is worshipped and glorified; he has spoken through the prophets." It is one path in which the use of existentialist language, the language of subjective human experience rather than doctrine, feels totally natural.

The Holy Spirit reminds us of some current cultural trends:

- the "spiritual but not religious" movement;
- Alcoholics Anonymous's relationship to a "higher power";
- depth psychologist Carl Jung's conception of the Holy Spirit as a mysterious force that brings about the unity of opposites, allowing the "transcendent" to manifest itself in time and space; and
- several recent novels about the thin line between spiritual ecstasy and sexual ecstasy (e.g.,

Mariette in Ecstasy by Ron Hansen; *The Well* by Catherine Chanter).

THE HOLY SPIRIT ACCORDING TO LUKE

The New Testament contains many passages about the Holy Spirit, but few so dramatic as those describing Pentecost and the conversion of Paul in the Acts of the Apostles, Luke's narrative of the life of the earliest church.

Nearly all the references in the early chapters of Acts associate the Holy Spirit with *power*. In his story of Jesus's last appearance to the apostles, Jesus says, "You will receive power when the Holy Spirit has come upon you; and you will be my witnesses in Jerusalem, in all Judea and Samaria, and to the ends of the earth" (Acts 1:8). The apostles, at least one of whom had denied even knowing Jesus and apparently all of whom had scattered in fear after the crucifixion, suddenly felt empowered to speak boldly to the world, despite the threat—and actuality—of arrest and execution. This is not your Aquarian spirit of "mystic, crystal revelations" of "harmony and understanding, sympathy and trust abounding." This is about power, the power to act boldly in spreading the gospel and the power to heal and perform "signs."

The church dates its inception not from the birth or death of Jesus or even from the resurrection event, but from the outpouring of the Holy Spirit at the first Feast of Pentecost after the resurrection experiences. The event is one of power and the onlookers interpret it as drunkenness:

> When the day of Pentecost had come, they were all together in one place. And suddenly from heaven there came a sound like the rush of a violent wind, and it filled the entire house where they were sitting. Divided tongues, as of fire, appeared among them, and a tongue rested on each of them. All of them were filled with the Holy Spirit and began to speak in other languages, as the Spirit gave them ability. . . . But Peter, standing with the eleven, raised his voice and addressed them, "Men of Judea and all who live in Jerusalem, let this be known to you, and listen to what I say. Indeed, these are not drunk, as you suppose, for it is only nine o'clock in the morning. No, this is what was spoken through the prophet Joel: 'In the last days it will be, God declares, that I will pour out my Spirit upon all flesh, and your sons and your daughters shall prophesy, and your young men shall see visions, and your old men shall dream dreams.'" (Acts 2:1–4; 14–17)

The power of the Holy Spirit, Luke tells us, creates in those who receive it not only boldness but also the gifts of healing, signs, and wonders. It inspires them to practice a radical economics, as Jesus's followers decide to live communally, in an attempt at realizing the kingdom of God:

> [They prayed,] "And now, Lord, look at their threats, and grant to your servants to speak your word with all boldness, while you stretch out your hand to heal, and signs and wonders are performed through the name of your holy servant Jesus." When they had prayed, the place in which they were gathered together was shaken; and they were all filled with the Holy Spirit and spoke the word of God with boldness.
>
> Now the whole group of those who believed were of one heart and soul, and no one claimed private ownership of any possessions, but everything they owned was held in common. With great power the apostles gave their testimony to the resurrection of the Lord Jesus, and great grace was upon them all. There was not a needy person among them, for as many as owned lands or houses sold them and brought the proceeds of what was sold. They laid it at the apostles' feet, and it was distributed to each as any had need. (Acts 4:29–35)

As Karl Marx said centuries later, "From each according to his ability, to each according to his need."

The failures of these experiments—both that of the disciples and those of most attempts to date to realize Marx's vision—have a tragic dimension.

Another powerful story of the manifestation of the Spirit is Luke's recounting of the stoning of Stephen. Stephen had been chosen by the community as one of seven men to serve as spokespersons for the movement because he was a man "full of faith and the Holy Spirit" and of "grace and power." According to Luke, he did "great wonders and signs" among the people. But several groups, including the "synagogue of the Freedmen," charged Stephen with speaking blasphemous words against Moses and God. They stirred up the elders, the scribes, and the people to seize Stephen and bring him before the council.

Stephen was clearly "in the Spirit," as even the council noted that his face was "like the face of an angel." His captors grilled him, nonetheless, and Stephen responded by recounting the history of the Israelites from the time of Abraham to the time of Solomon, ending with a charge: "You are forever opposing the Holy Spirit, just as your ancestors used to do. . . . And now you have become [the] betrayers and murderers" of the Righteous One (Acts 7:51–52).

The council became enraged and "ground their teeth at Stephen":

But filled with the Holy Spirit, he gazed into heaven and saw the glory of God and Jesus standing at the right hand of God. "Look," he said, "I see the heavens opened and the Son of Man standing at the right hand of God!" But they covered their ears, and with a loud shout all rushed together against him. Then they dragged him out of the city and began to stone him; and the witnesses laid their coats at the feet of a young man named Saul. While they were stoning Stephen, he prayed, "Lord Jesus, receive my spirit." Then he knelt down and cried out in a loud voice, "Lord, do not hold this sin against them." When he had said this, he died. And Saul approved of their killing him. (Acts 7:55–8:1)

Saul, of course, was soon to become Paul after his own dramatic spiritual encounter. On the road to Damascus, while pursuing followers of "the Way" so that he could tie them up and take them before the council in Jerusalem, Saul suddenly experienced a light from heaven that blinded him, and he fell to the ground.

At least, this is Luke's version of the story in the book of Acts. The very broadest outlines are affirmed by Paul himself in Galatians 1 and 1 Corinthians 15, but Paul gives us none of the detail, leaving us to wonder about the facticity of the details in Luke's story.

In any event, Luke tells us that Saul hears the voice of a man claiming to be Jesus, who tells him to go to Damascus. Saul does not recover his sight for three days.

In the meantime, a man named Ananias in Damascus also hears the voice of the Lord, which tells him to go to the place where Saul is staying and lay his hands on him so that he might regain his sight:

> So Ananias went and entered the house. He laid his hands on Saul and said, "Brother Saul, the Lord Jesus, who appeared to you on your way here, has sent me so that you may regain your sight and be filled with the Holy Spirit." And immediately something like scales fell from his eyes, and his sight was restored. Then he got up and was baptized, and after taking some food, he regained his strength. For several days he was with the disciples in Damascus, and immediately he began to proclaim Jesus in the synagogues, saying, "He is the Son of God." (Acts 9:17–20)

Whatever we make of Luke's colorful detail, the fact remains that Saul, who had never met Jesus when he was alive, is transformed from a leading persecutor of Jesus's followers to the man who constantly risked his life to spread the Way among the Gentiles, in effect becoming the father of Christianity as we know it.

The Holy Spirit According to Paul (Tillich)

What does the existentialist Tillich make of the Holy Spirit? To Tillich, ordinary life is constantly subject to what he calls *ambiguity*: that is to say, because of our existential estrangement, the positive and the negative elements in us are always thoroughly mixed and inseparable. This is, of course, borne out by all the various schools of depth psychology. As Tillich says, our self-integration is always threatened and often destroyed by disintegration. We inevitably lose our centeredness from one day to the next. Our creativity and growth constantly come up against their limitations, creating ennui or frustration or despair. Our freedom to act is always bound by our finitude. We all know these things, although we may not express them as abstractly as Tillich. We call them the "human condition," and it drives us to seek some sort of healing, most often, in our time, through psychotherapy.

The closest I personally ever came to this kind of despair was in my late twenties. I was working as the Physicians Relations Representative at a Blue Cross Blue Shield plan. My job was essentially to be a "flak catcher," to use Tom Wolfe's evocative term. I sometimes described my job as "getting beat up by doctors." In my second year in the job, I began to develop intermittent abdominal pain so intense that I would go to the ER, where they would give me Demerol; I would sleep for a day and then go back to catching flak. At one point, I was admitted to the hospital. Since my job involved traveling around the state to call on doctors, my episodes sometimes occurred at night in motels in unfamiliar towns. My mother came to visit, and I can still picture her, standing on the front lawn, unable to think of anything helpful to say, but with tears running down her cheeks. It was the most healing thing that happened to me. As Rachel Held Evans said, "We are called to enter into one another's pain, anoint it as holy, and stick around no matter what the outcome."[1]

In his magnum opus, *Systematic Theology*, Tillich identifies three important symbols that all point to the way out of this ambiguous life—Tillich calls this way the *quest for unambiguous life*: (1) the Spiritual Presence (the term is Tillich's attempt to rehabilitate the notion of the Holy Spirit); (2) the kingdom of God; and (3) eternal life. They are closely related. Eternal life is not life extended forever but life in the Spirit. And the kingdom of God is what life in society would be if we lived unambiguously in the Spirit.

But what would unambiguous life in the Spirit look like? What Tillich has to say philosophically and theologically is too abstract for most of us, but we all know what sublimity feels like, even if we can't say precisely what it is. As Justice Potter Stewart famously said about hard-core pornography, "Perhaps I could never succeed in intelligibly [defining it]. But I know it when I see it."

Commentators, including Santayana, have given us a hint by pointing out that religion has more in common with art than with metaphysics or doctrine. For many, the touchstone is music (in my case, the music of Johann Sebastian Bach). Like many, I often get a sublime sense of unambiguous life when listening to the St. Matthew Passion or Albinoni's "Adagio in G Minor" or Leonard Cohen's "Hallelujah." People talk of being "transported" by music, and that is as concrete a word as any for the experience of unambiguous life.

For others, the experience of the unambiguously sublime is triggered by architecture. On my sole trip to Chartres cathedral with my wife, Eloise, I was stunned to feel tears spring to my eyes, and this verse from Job sprang into my head: "I have uttered what I did not understand, things too wonderful for me, which I did not know" (Job 42:3). When I looked up the verse later, I was reminded that this experience is what leads Job to exclaim, "I had heard of you by the hearing of the ear, but now my eye sees you; therefore I despise myself, and repent in dust and ashes" (Job 42:5–6).

Another analog for unambiguous life in the Spirit is sexual union. Because the Spirit "breaks into" the ambiguous structure of our ordinary life, it is, Tillich says, often experienced as ecstasy. It is little wonder that many have noted its similarity to sexual ecstasy. In sexual ecstasy, we lose our sense of the ambiguous nature of the other person and become enraptured with our vision of them as unambiguously desirable. Later, to put it delicately, we may find it difficult to recapture the unambiguous quality of that vision. Similarly, we eventually lose our contact with the Spiritual Presence, along with our compelling picture of the kingdom of God and our sense of living in the light of eternity. That is the human condition.

The Song of Songs celebrates the experience of unambiguous erotic love:

My beloved is to me a bag of myrrh that lies between my breasts. My beloved is to me a cluster of henna blossoms in the vineyards of En-gedi. Ah, you are beautiful, my love; ah, you are beautiful; your eyes are doves. Ah, you are beautiful, my beloved, truly lovely. (Song 1:13–16)

I found him whom my soul loves. I held him, and would not let him go until I brought him into my mother's house, and into the chamber of her that conceived me. (Song 3:4)

Your lips are like a crimson thread, and your mouth is lovely. Your cheeks are like halves of a pomegranate behind your veil. . . . Your two breasts are like two fawns, twins of a gazelle, that feed among the lilies. Until the day breathes and the shadows flee, I will hasten to the mountain of myrrh and the hill of frankincense. You are altogether beautiful, my love; there is no flaw in you. (Song 4:3–7)

No flaw? Really? We've all been there.

Song of Songs is one of two books in the Bible that does not mention God. (The other is Esther.) How then did a book of erotic poetry end up in the canon? The answer is that it was supposedly intended as an allegory for God's love for Israel. Really? No, of course not. It's a book of erotic poetry. I know it when I see it. But no matter. It is still a depiction of unambiguous life.

Years ago, when I was a young probation officer in Dutchess County, New York, the District Attorney's office raided the Castalia Foundation, Timothy Leary's mansion in Millbrook where he entertained guests, many of them celebrities, who wished to be initiated into the psychedelic experience through LSD. I was as curious as the next person, so I decided to walk up the carriage road to the foundation's mansion and ask if I could stay overnight. (Yes, it was a flagrant boundary violation of my role as a probation officer who might soon be asked to write presentence investigations of the arrestees. Ah, youth.) A guest said he'd have to ask Tim, so while I waited twenty minutes for that to happen, I stood and watched a handsome young man and a beautiful young woman peel potatoes. The potatoes were clearly of secondary interest. They gazed at each other with wide, rapturous grins, and they nearly literally glowed. Like Stephen, they had the faces of angels. I interpreted their intensity to be a combination of their obvious attraction to each other and, perhaps more importantly, the feeling they seemed to have that they were sharing secret psychedelic knowledge, unknown to the rest of us. They were clearly participating in unambiguous life.

(Incidentally, fortunately or unfortunately for me, Tim said no. An outrageous risk-taker, Leary apparently decided that he needed to draw the line at inviting a law enforcement officer to join him. Months later, I finally had my first psychedelic experience and knew firsthand the feeling of seeing the world unambiguously. My biggest revelation: "You can always get higher, Danny!" You had to be there.)

(NB: The psychedelic experience can also be unadulterated hell, as Danny will attest. *It should never be undertaken without the presence of an experienced guide.* Take very seriously the fact that Aldous Huxley called his book *Heaven and Hell.*)

So where does faith come in? Tillich says that faith, contrary to being "belief in something for which there is no evidence," is precisely the state of being grasped by the Spiritual Presence and overwhelmed by the experience of unambiguous life. Note the similarity to Jung's conception of a mysterious force that brings about the unity of opposites, the transcendent and the temporal. It is precisely the psychedelic experience.

The Spiritual Presence expresses itself not only as faith but also as *agape*, the New Testament Greek word for "unambiguous love," which draws us into the unity of unambiguous life. But neither faith nor *agape* love are possible for the human spirit alone. They are always experienced as given to us or revealed to us.

We've come a long way from the creedal formulation of the Spirit as "the giver of life, who proceeds from the Father and the Son, and who with the Father and the Son is worshipped and glorified, and who has spoken through the prophets." Once again, we have seen a common path into Christianity that relies on experience rather than doctrine and that can perhaps move beyond inwardness to a "religionless Christianity" that aspires to create a Beloved Community, or the kingdom of God.

8

THE GIFT

We have already noted the intimate connection between our first two paths, the kingdom of God and life in the Spirit. The kingdom is the social manifestation of life in the Spirit.

There is also a connection between the kingdom of God and our third path: the gift of forgiveness. We noted Jesus's formulation that one must "turn" or repent to enter the kingdom. The result of this turning is sometimes expressed by Jesus as entry into the kingdom, at other times as forgiveness of sin.

Luke tells the story of "the woman who was a sinner":

One of the Pharisees asked Jesus to eat with him, and he went into the Pharisee's house and took his place at the table. And a woman in the city, who was a sinner, having learned that he was eating in the Pharisee's house, brought an alabaster jar of ointment. She stood behind him at his feet, weeping, and began to bathe his feet with her tears and to dry them with her hair. Then she continued kissing his feet and anointing them with the ointment. Now when the Pharisee who had invited him saw it, he said to himself, "If this man were a prophet, he would have known who and what kind of woman this is who is touching him—that she is a sinner." Jesus spoke up and said to him, "Simon, I have something to say to you." "Teacher," he replied, "speak." "A certain creditor had two debtors; one owed five hundred denarii, and the other fifty. When they could not pay, he canceled the debts for both of them. Now which of them will love him more?" Simon answered, "I suppose the one for whom he canceled the greater debt." And Jesus said to him, "You have judged rightly." Then turning toward the woman, he said to Simon, "Do you see this woman? I entered your house; you gave me no water for my feet, but she has bathed my feet with her tears and dried them with her hair. You gave me no kiss, but from the time I came in she has not stopped kissing my feet. You did not anoint my head with oil, but she has anointed my feet with ointment. Therefore, I tell you, her sins, which were many, have been forgiven; hence she has shown great love. But the one to whom little is forgiven, loves little." Then he said to her, "Your sins are forgiven." But those who were at the table with him began to say among themselves, "Who is this who even forgives sins?"

And he said to the woman, "Your faith has saved you; go
in peace." (Luke 7:36–50 and parallels)

This story raises an obvious question. How could
she—or we—dare to accept such acceptance? Is this not
just an act of self-forgiveness, yet another example of
greater and deeper alienation (sin), of unjustified self-
reliance and pathetic self-centeredness?

Kierkegaard, with his typical subtlety, says that, on
the contrary, to *refuse* forgiveness is, paradoxically, the
sinful act. It is the refusal to see ourselves from any
point of view other than our own pathetic self-reliance.

The woman in the story is *experiencing* her own forgiveness, although she may not have called it that until
Jesus did. Note that the woman has not relinquished
her vivid awareness of her alienation. Her tears testify
to that. She is conscious that she is "accepted *in spite of*
being unacceptable," to use Tillich's phrase.

Note also that her acceptance of acceptance created an outburst of ecstatic love. A special case of that
ecstatic love is the creation of our own ability to forgive others when we experience ourselves as forgiven.
When white supremacist Dylann Roof walked into
Mother Emanuel AME Church in Charleston, South
Carolina, sat in a circle with African American Bible
students for an hour, then calmly shot nine of them

dead, the world was stunned. If ever there was an unforgivable crime, surely this was it. But in the next few days, several survivors—friends and relatives of the murdered—came forward to say that they forgave Roof.

Was this crazy? Were these people simply carrying out a moralistic demand of their religion that could not possibly hold up over time? Surely, as many people at the time observed, natural justice does not require such a disproportionate response.

Or was it instead that they literally could not help themselves, because they too had experienced the grace of being accepted in spite of being unacceptable?

There are enough questions raised by such stories to keep skeptics and Christians alike from comfortably relating to them. Chief among them is the question many of us feel: "Unacceptable? Really? We mess up occasionally, but we don't feel unacceptable. We're more or less like everybody else—basically pretty good but also 'human.'"

Kierkegaard knew that his fellow Danish Christians were miles away from being able to relate to the story. Their Christianity was too anemic. They probably had not done much dramatic sinning. They were too nice. Perhaps this is what Luther was referring to when he said, "Sin boldly!" As Jesus said, "The one to whom little is forgiven, loves little" (Luke 7:47).

Is this an invitation to sin? As Paul said, "May it never be!" More likely, it's an invitation to take what Alcoholics Anonymous calls a "searching and fearless moral inventory of ourselves," including asking ourselves why, if we're so OK, do we sometimes fall into anxiety, depression, and even despair and search out professional help? Tillich draws the parallel between psychotherapy and the gift of ultimate forgiveness. Critical to psychotherapeutic healing is acceptance by the therapist. The fact that the therapist is another person is crucial so that we are not simply accepting ourselves.

The difference between psychotherapy and what we have called the gift of forgiveness lies in the ultimacy of the latter. That is why we describe forgiveness as something received "from God."

We may visit a psychotherapist because forces that are beyond our conscious control are determining our mood. For "no good reason," we find ourselves thrown into a deep depression or unbearable anxiety or sudden panic or mania, and we realize that we need professional help to sort it out and try to remove it, either through medication or increased self-insight.

We may not find psychotherapy useful, however, if we experience our guilt as irremovable because we know we are totally unable to live up to our own moral

code. We may not benefit from therapy if our guilt stems
from the fact that we have deeply injured a loved one or
if we chronically put our own interests before the legitimate interests of others. We may find it irrelevant to
seek out a psychotherapist if our problem is not *feelings*
of cowardice but actual cowardice—with actual consequences. Psychotherapy may help some with teasing
out of the unconscious or neurotic components of these
problems, but in the end, what we need is forgiveness.

Forgiveness from the people we have injured will
help enormously, but it will be useless unless we can
also experience what a self-help guru would probably
call "self-forgiveness," but that we know must be far less
ambiguous than that. To forgive ourselves is slippery
territory for obvious reasons. We must instead "find
ourselves forgiven" by what we symbolically call "the
grace of God." This, too, is subject to gaping ambiguity, of course, as it can easily mask what is really self-
forgiveness. In the end, accepting forgiveness takes the
courage of faith.

Nadia Bolz-Weber, the heavily tattooed recovering
addict and founder of the House for All Sinners and
Saints, a Lutheran congregation in Denver, describes
the grace she received like this: "Getting sober never
felt like I had pulled myself up by my own spiritual
bootstraps. It felt instead like I was on one path toward

destruction and God pulled me off it by the scruff of my collar, me hopelessly kicking and flailing and saying, 'Screw you. I'll take the destruction please.' God looked at tiny, little red-faced me and said, 'that's adorable,' and then plunked me down on an entirely different path."[1]

Once again, we have looked at a path that begins in experience rather than in doctrine and that hopefully ends in our commitment to the vision of the kingdom of God in a religionless world.

9

CHRIST IN ME?

We have become familiar—too familiar—with glib notions such as "our inner child" or "the mom within." But Paul tells us he has experienced the "Christ within." This is our fourth path into Christian life that is based on experience rather than doctrine.

The letter to the Colossians boldly claims that "the mystery that has been hidden throughout the ages and generations but has now been revealed to his saints" (Hart says, "made manifest in his holy ones") is "Christ in you, the hope of glory" (Col 1:26 and 27).

Scholars are virtually unanimous that Colossians, which the salutation claims is from Paul and Timothy, was actually written not by Paul but rather "in the spirit of Paul," apparently a common practice in those days. The reasons for the conclusion that the letter is not actually from Paul are beyond my education, but suffice it to say, they stem from an analysis of style, language, and theology. But "Christ in you" appears in the genuinely Pauline letters as well, particularly in his letter to the Romans: "But you are not in the flesh; you are in the Spirit, since the Spirit of God dwells in you. Anyone who does not have the Spirit of Christ does not belong to him. But if *Christ is in you*, though the body is dead because of sin, the Spirit is life because of righteousness" (Rom 8:9–10; emphasis mine). (See also 1 Cor 3:16, 2 Cor 13:5, and Gal 4:19.)

Paul in the above passage equates "Christ in you" with the "Spirit of God in you" and the "Spirit of Christ in you." That's helpful. Maybe "Christ in you" isn't a lot different from what we called the path via the Holy Spirit, except for the felt relationship with our image of the risen Christ.

More often than not, Paul speaks of our being "in Christ" rather than Christ being in us. The two phrases seem to mean the same thing: a semimystical union of Christ and us.

The key to understanding Paul's notion of living in Christ is the parallel notion that he alternately calls "dying to the flesh" or "dying to sin" or "dying to the law" or being "crucified with Christ": "For through the law I died to the law, so that I might live to God. I have been crucified with Christ; and it is no longer I who live, but it is Christ who lives in me. And the life

I now live in the flesh I live by faith in the Son of God, who loved me and gave himself for me" (Gal 2:19–20).

One night, in probably 1959 or 1960, Danny and I sat on the front steps of Adams House and had one of our recurring midnight talks. Somehow the topic turned to religion, and I was apparently saying something about the demands of Christianity, dying to "the world" and so on. I must have mentioned the story of the rich young man whom Jesus tells to sell all that he has, give the money to the poor, and join Jesus on the road. Danny, with his keen nose for hypocrisy, said, "But you don't do that." Thanks, Danny.

Like most mainstream Christians in those days, I had heard sermons about how Jesus's demand was particular to that man because his wealth was his hang-up, and the rest of us should look to our own hang-ups; but that night I wasn't buying it, probably because I knew Danny would keep me honest. I don't remember what I did say, but today I'm remembering what Paul said:

> I do not understand my own actions. For I do not do what I want, but I do the very thing I hate. Now if I do what I do not want, I agree that the law is good. But in fact it is no longer I that do it, but sin that dwells within me. For I know that nothing good dwells within me—that is, in my flesh. I can will what is right, but I

cannot do it. For I do not do the good I want, but the evil I do not want is what I do. Now if I do what I do not want, it is no longer I that do it, but sin that dwells within me. (Rom 7:15–20)

Add to this Tillich's observation that all life decisions are ambiguous, and the difficulty becomes overwhelming. Even if we take our narrow self-interest out of these decisions (easy to do in the case of my "wealth" at the time), the legitimacy of any ethical decision still remains ambiguous. Should my father really take his son out of school and give all his wealth to the poor—and then do what? Should my teachers do the same, thereby making it impossible for them and their families to subsist in Cambridge? On the other hand, how much attention should we pay to the fact that our self-serving tendency to take the easy way out will probably guarantee that we remain in the status quo? All this is what Paul would call "the law," parsing all the ethical pros and cons. Being in the law is not bad in itself, but being in the law is not being in Christ.

A few years later we would be faced with a more urgent question: whether to avoid the draft and the war in Vietnam. Didn't the war seem senseless? Yes, but at twenty-five years old, could we really be sure that the government was wrong in claiming the war would prevent neighboring countries from falling into authoritarian hands? Wasn't it immoral to, in effect, duck and let the guy behind us in the draft line take the bullet? Didn't the young antiwar activists, with their apparent certainty that the war was immoral, sometimes sound self-serving and hypocritical? Many ended up taking the route I took: with this much moral ambiguity, my default position became to preserve my life. "Sin dwelling in me?"; it was certainly an element in my decision, regardless of the rightness or wrongness of my conclusion.

Years later, my lovely daughter—and only child—became, as we used to say in a more honest era, a child from a "broken home." I broke it. I knew the literature on the effects of divorce on children, but I convinced myself that Esther would probably be OK *if she lived with me*. In the end, she didn't want to live with me, and she wasn't OK. Nor would she have been OK if she had lived with me; her mom did a much better job than I would have. Today, sometimes the generosity and depth of Esther's forgiveness is almost unbearable. And I am proud to report that, after a monumental struggle, Esther is now a "wounded healer," helping others find their way.

As Paul said, "I can will what is right, but I cannot do it. For I do not do the good I want, but the evil I do not want is what I do." How do I dare write a book about the gospel? It certainly isn't because I have lived it. But if sin, alienation, dwells within me, is it possible that Christ might one day dwell within me?

One night after working on a draft of this book, I woke up in a state of high anxiety. I had dreamed that I came home to find a car in our driveway with a bedraggled, distressed young woman and three small children inside. It was clear to me that the mother was desperate. They had nowhere to go. It was up to me to take them into our home. I began to temporize and think of all the reasons that could not possibly work. When I woke up in a panic, it was clear to me that the dream was accusing me of being a total fraud—writing a book about Christianity when I couldn't even take the simple, sincere step of taking this woman into my home.

Yes, of course, there's a case to be made that taking them into my home really couldn't have worked. That's the ambiguity of all decisions, the ambiguity of "the law." But my first response was an unambiguous "oh, my God, no!" That's complacency "dwelling in me," unwillingness to leave my comfort zone dwelling in me, resentment of inconvenience dwelling in me, worry about how the neighbors would perceive the situation dwelling in me. I confess that if I had been that Samaritan on the road to Jericho, my first instinct might well have been to pass by on the other side. I would have done that in my dream if she weren't sitting in my driveway.

Sometimes, fleetingly, I'm aware that Christ dwells in me too. I can't control that or produce it on demand, but I can accept it—or not. As some anonymous sage said, I can't make the light, but I can choose whether or not to walk in it. I cannot bring about my own resurrection—my own "living in Christ"—but I can dare to "die to the flesh," as Paul says, because I am inspired by Christ, his life, death, and resurrection. We take this leap of faith in the hope that Christ will dwell unambiguously in us and we in him.

What is the "flesh" that Paul urges us to die to? In his letter to the Philippians, Paul provides a clue to what he means by dying to the flesh; he means in part renouncing all those things that, as we say these days, make us "feel good about ourselves," all the things that in the world's view, and our own, bring honor, respect, prestige, and reward. In short, it means counting all gain in this world of flesh and blood as loss:

> If anyone else has reason to be confident in the flesh, I have more: circumcised on the eighth day, a member of the people of Israel, of the tribe of Benjamin, a Hebrew born of Hebrews; as to the law, a Pharisee; as to zeal, a

persecutor of the church; as to righteousness under the law, blameless. Yet whatever gains I had, these I have come to regard as loss because of Christ. More than that, I regard everything as loss because of the surpassing value of knowing Christ Jesus my Lord. For his sake I have suffered the loss of all things, and I regard them as rubbish, [Hart says, "I regard them as excrement"] in order that I may gain Christ. (Phil 3:4–8)

Is the "flesh," as many think, the sensual life of the body? Paul lays out the sins of the flesh: "Now the works of the flesh are obvious: fornication, impurity, licentiousness, idolatry, sorcery, enmities, strife, jealousy, anger, quarrels, dissensions, factions, envy, drunkenness, carousing, and things like these" (Gal 5:19–21).

Sure enough, some of the "works of the flesh" do have to do with the body, at least in part: fornication; impurity (I guess); licentiousness; to some extent, drunkenness and carousing. But most of Paul's list has nothing to do with the body: idolatry, sorcery, enmities, strife, jealousy, anger, quarrels, dissensions, factions, and envy. So "flesh" seems to refer to our corrupt world of flesh and blood and to any behavior that is not "in Christ." In fact, in the previous passage from Philippians, the world of the flesh that Paul renounces includes not only sins but also religious observance (circumcision), identification with a tribe of Israel, the righteousness of a Pharisee, religious zeal, and blamelessness under the law. All this is excrement compared to being "in Christ."

Paul identifies this "death to the flesh" with (adult) baptism and "newness of life":

> Do you not know that all of us who have been baptized into Christ Jesus were baptized into his death? Therefore we have been buried with him by baptism into death, so that, just as Christ was raised from the dead by the glory of the Father, so we too might walk in *newness of life*. For if we have been united with him in a death like his, we will certainly be united with him in a resurrection like his. We know that our old self was crucified with him so that the body of sin might be destroyed, and we might no longer be enslaved to sin. For whoever has died is freed from sin. But if we have died with Christ, we believe that we will also live with him. (Rom 6:3–8)

This newness of life is what Tillich calls the "New Being" and what the rest of us call "transformation"—of ourselves and, to the extent possible, our world.

10

BRINGING IT ALL BACK HOME

As I write this, it is Palm Sunday (aka Passion Sunday), and today Eloise and I went to services at our little country church, St. John the Evangelist Episcopal Church in Barrytown, New York. Our vicar, Mary Grace Williams, led the service and preached a beautiful sermon called "Why Did He Go?," meaning why did Jesus go to Jerusalem when he must have known that it would probably end in his death? Good question. Mary Grace wisely chose not to speculate about the answer but rather leave it percolating in our heads.

As I listened to the sermon and the liturgy, it became clearer than usual to me that "religionless Christianity" is only relevant to a segment of Christians. I remembered Tillich, in one of his sermons, saying he knew a woman who didn't need theology; she embodied it. I used to take that to mean that she didn't need doctrinal theology. Today, it seemed clear to me that perhaps she didn't need "religionless Christianity" either. She already knew what in religious observance was wheat and what was chaff.

There was plenty of "religion" in the service. We read aloud a prayer Episcopalians call a "Collect": "Mercifully grant that we may walk in the way of his suffering, and also share in his resurrection; through Jesus Christ our Lord, who lives and reigns with you and the Holy Spirit, one God, for ever and ever. Amen." Did the congregation take the last part of this literally? Did anyone picture the Father, Son, and Holy Spirit "living and reigning" together, like Louis XVI and Marie Antoinette? Hardly.

When Shakespeare asks if he should compare you to a summer's day, does anyone really think of what it would feel like to be "less windy"? Poetic—or, if you prefer, symbolic—language exists in a world of its own, only mysteriously related to what we generally call the "real world," the world of flesh and blood.

The first time I felt I fully understood what a poem is and how it works was when, as a young man, I listened to Bob Dylan's "Desolation Row." "They're selling postcards of the hanging, they're painting the passports brown." Who's painting passports brown and why would anyone do such a crazy thing? We'll never know—Dylan didn't know—and it's irrelevant. This is what "Desolation Row" *feels* like. It is the same poetic connection that Santayana was talking about. Religion as sublime poetry, not pseudoscience.

Even when we read the Nicene Creed this morning— "Through [Jesus Christ] all things were made. For us and for our salvation, he came down from heaven: by the power of the Holy Spirit he became incarnate from the Virgin Mary, and was made man"—it was hard to imagine that anyone in the church was picturing that truly weird-sounding process: Christ helping out with creation, then "coming down," then somehow becoming incarnate in Mary's womb.

When we prayed for healing for specific persons, did people picture a sort of magical divine intervention? Or, as Tillich says, were they instead taking part in a spiritual act of elevating the content of their wishes and hopes into the realm of the Holy Spirit? My guess is that the breakdown in the congregation was probably fifty-fifty. Consider the fact that people generally do not count the many instances when the prayed-for outcome does not occur. This would seem to suggest that these people were not praying for magic so much as expressing their hopes and fears *sub specie aeternitatis*, in the light of eternity, or perhaps, as my wife, Eloise, pointed out, standing together in solidarity.

In a way, I guess that has been my point all along, that our four paths (and many others) are on a different plane altogether from statements of belief. What was different on this Passion Sunday was that it seemed clearer to me that for many people in the church that day, this didn't really need saying.

Apologetic theology is situated at the borders of Christianity. It is a response to people who have expressed their alienation—whether aggressively or searchingly—in questions and concerns about the border between faith and reason. The only import of such theology lies in the fact that, as Tillich says, these questions can be a stumbling block for skeptics, which is to say, for many of us, both inside and outside the church. The goal of apologetic theology is to clear away the brush and make it possible to think more clearly about the true boundaries of faith. Not that thinking clearly about faith is the essential thing. But *not* thinking *falsely* about faith *is* essential, lest we get misled into an alien formulation of our faith that we and the world can no longer believe in.

But Bonhoeffer was speaking of an even deeper reason that it is necessary for Christianity to shed religion. Religion, as such, has lost its power to grasp many of us where we live. This was dramatically clear in Nazi Germany, and it is increasingly evident in most of the United States today.

If we are to reimagine Christianity, it is essential to remember that it isn't something we think or something we're a member of; it's something we live. That's why it is that my dear friend Jewish-atheist Danny can be a better Christian than I am. Franciscan friar Richard Rohr put it this way: "Christianity is a lifestyle—a way of being in the world that is simple, nonviolent, shared, and loving. However, we made it into an established 'religion' (and all that goes with that) and avoided the lifestyle change itself. One could be warlike, greedy, racist, selfish, and vain in most of Christian history, and still believe that Jesus Christ is one's 'personal Lord and Savior.' . . . The world has no time for such silliness anymore. The suffering on Earth is too great."[1]

One final irony from Passion Sunday: I was asked by Mary Grace to read one of the scripture passages at the following week's Easter service. It turned out to be from Paul's first letter to the Corinthians:

> If for this life only we have hoped in Christ, we are of all people most to be pitied.
>
> But in fact Christ has been raised from the dead, the first fruits of those who have died. For since death came through a human being, the resurrection of the dead has also come through a human being; for as all die in Adam, so all will be made alive in Christ. But each in his own order: Christ the first fruits, then at his coming those who belong to Christ. Then comes the end,

when he hands over the kingdom to God the Father, after he has destroyed every ruler and every authority and power. For he must reign until he has put all his enemies under his feet. The last enemy to be destroyed is death. (1 Cor 15:19–26)

Could there be a starker example of the sort of literalistic passage the New Atheists understandably like to highlight? Is this Paul's attempt at "science" more than a millennium and a half before science as we know it existed? Not likely.

On the other hand, the young John Updike, hardly a scientist, makes the point that only the literal resurrection is "monstrous" enough to have the power to transform us.

The power of the monstrosity of the crucifixion and a literal resurrection are undeniable. I confess that even I am gripped in a different way—yes, a more powerful way—when I picture Jesus literally rising from the dead. But can we not also feel the power of Paul's more poetic vision, a vision that he can't get out of his head, an ecstatic vision of what it means to die to the world and live in Christ, to live in eternal life?

Perhaps the religious imagination operates on two tracks, the literal and the symbolic, and the mark of the best symbolism is that it convinces us that it is real.

Perhaps all we can do is say with Mary Oliver, "If you were there, it was all those things. If you can imagine it, it is all those things."[2] Perhaps religionless Christianity is what we are called to live seven days a week, while religion is what we do on Sunday. Perhaps religious ritual is meant to clear our heads and hearts for the real religionless work of participating in the kingdom of God through being open to being grasped by that vision, or by being receptive to the Holy Spirit, or by courageously and humbly accepting forgiveness, or by staying open to the Christ in us, or yet another path.

"Concluding Unscientific Postscript"

At the outset, I cited the statistics on the dwindling numbers of mainline Protestants and the growing number of "Nones," people who claim no religion.

A few weeks ago, Bishop Mary Glasspool of the Episcopal Diocese of New York visited our little parish, preached, and met after church with the board. Several board members expressed concern that our parish had an aging population and was possibly aging out of existence. Bishop Glasspool had a surprising response. She said, "You're not alone. But I don't worry about the institutional church dying out." She cited the words of Jesus, when he was told that his mother and brothers were looking for him: "'Who is my mother, and who are my brothers?' And pointing to his disciples, he said, 'Here are my mother and my brothers! For whoever does the will of my Father in heaven is my brother and sister and mother'" (Matt 12:48–50 and parallels).

She said, "There will always be people in the world who embody the spirit of Christ and inspire others to do likewise, even if the church as we know it dies out completely."

Amen, Bishop Glasspool.

FURTHER READING

Altizer, Thomas J. J., and William Hamilton. *Radical Theology and the Death of God*. Indianapolis: Bobbs-Merrill, 1966.

Bolz-Weber, Nadia. *Pastrix: The Cranky, Beautiful Faith of a Sinner and Saint*. Nashville: Jericho, 2013.

Bonhoeffer, Dietrich. *Letters and Papers from Prison*. Edited by Eberhard Bethge. New York: Touchstone, 2011.

Bultmann, Rudolf, and five critics. *Kerygma and Myth*. Edited by Hans Werner Bartsch. Translated by Reginald H. Fuller. New York: Harper & Row, 1961.

Caputo, John D. *How to Read Kierkegaard*. New York: W. W. Norton, 2008.

Comte-Sponville, André. *The Little Book of Atheist Spirituality*. New York: Penguin, 2008.

Cox, Harvey. *When Jesus Came to Harvard: Making Moral Choices Today*. Boston: Houghton Mifflin, 2004.

Evans, Rachel Held. *Searching for Sunday: Loving, Leaving, and Finding the Church*. Nashville: Nelson, 2015.

Harris, Sam. *The End of Faith*. New York: W. W. Norton, 2004.

———. *Letter to a Christian Nation*. New York: Knopf, 2006.

Hart, David Bentley. *The New Testament: A Translation*. New Haven, CT: Yale University Press, 2017.

Hitchens, Christopher. *God Is Not Great: How Religion Poisons Everything*. New York: Twelve, 2007.

Kierkegaard, Søren. *The Concept of Anxiety*. Translated by Alastair Hannay. New York: Liveright, 2014.

———. "An Edifying Discourse." In *Training in Christianity*. Translated by Walter Lowrie. Princeton, NJ: Princeton University Press, 1941.

———. *Papers and Journals: A Selection*. Edited and translated by Alastair Hannay. New York: Penguin, 1996.

———. *The Sickness Unto Death: A Christian Psychological Exposition for Upbuilding and Awakening*. Translated by Howard Hong and Edna Hong. Princeton, NJ: Princeton University Press, 1983.

———. *Works of Love*. Translated by Howard Hong and Edna Hong. Princeton, NJ: Princeton University Press, 1998.

King, Martin Luther, Jr. *Where Do We Go from Here: Chaos or Community?* Boston: Beacon, 1968.

Marsh, Charles. *Strange Glory: A Life of Dietrich Bonhoeffer*. New York: Knopf, 2014.

Murdoch, Iris. *The Sovereignty of Good*. London: Routledge & Kegan Paul, 1976.

Otto, Rudolf. *The Idea of the Holy*. Translated by John W. Harvey. New York: Oxford University Press, 1958.

Santayana, George. *Reason in Religion*. Vol. 7, bk. 3, *Life of Reason*, edited by Marianna S. Wokeck and Martin A. Coleman. Cambridge, MA: MIT Press, 2014.

Stoppard, Tom. *The Hard Problem*. London: Faber & Faber, 2015.

Taylor, Jill Bolte. *My Stroke of Insight*. New York: Penguin, 2009.

Thurman, Howard. *Jesus and the Disinherited*. Boston: Beacon, 1996.

Tillich, Paul. *The Courage to Be*. New Haven, CT: Yale University Press, 1952.

———. *Systematic Theology*. 3 vols. Chicago: University of Chicago Press, 1951–63.

Vermes, Geza. *The Real Jesus: Then and Now*. Minneapolis: Fortress, 2010.

Weil, Simone. *Waiting for God*. New York: Putnam, 1941.

Wright, Robert. *Why Buddhism Is True*. New York: Simon & Schuster, 2017.

Zuckerman, Phil. *Living the Secular Life: New Answers to Old Questions*. New York: Penguin, 2015.

NOTES

Introduction

1 Dietrich Bonhoeffer, *Letters and Papers from Prison*, ed. Eberhard Bethge (New York: Touchstone, 2011), 280.

Chapter 1

1 Jill Bolte Taylor, "My Stroke of Insight," filmed February 2008, TED video, https://www.youtube.com/watch?v=UyyjU8fzEYU.

2 Howard Thurman and Ronald Eyre, "An Interview with Howard Thurman and Ronald Eyre," *Theology Today* 38, no. 2 (1981): 208–13.

Chapter 3

1 Anne Lamott, *Plan B: Further Thoughts on Faith* (New York: Penguin, 2005), 179.

2 Max Ehrmann, "Desiderata," 1927, https://www.desiderata.com, public domain.

3 Søren Kierkegaard, *The Concept of Anxiety*, trans. Alastair Hannay (New York: Liveright, 2014), 51.

4 Søren Kierkegaard, *Papers and Journals: A Selection*, ed. and trans. Alastair Hannay (New York: Penguin, 1996), 102.

CHAPTER 4

1 George Santayana, *Reason in Religion*, vol. 7, bk. 3, *Life of Reason*, ed. Marianna S. Wokeck and Martin A. Coleman (Cambridge, MA: MIT Press, 2014), 5.

2 Santayana, 5.

3 Paul Tillich, *Systematic Theology*, vol. 1 (Chicago: University of Chicago Press, 1951), 235.

4 Harvey Cox, *When Jesus Came to Harvard: Making Moral Choices Today* (Boston: Houghton Mifflin, 2004), 302.

5 Ken Wilber, *One Taste: Daily Reflections on Integral Spirituality* (Boulder, CO: Shambhala, 2000), 21.

6 Rudolf Otto, *The Idea of the Holy*, trans. John W. Harvey (New York: Oxford University Press, 1970), 31.

7 NASA, accessed September 23, 2019, science.nasa.gov.

8 Richard Dawkins, *The Selfish Gene* (Oxford: Oxford University Press, 1976), 24–26.

9 Charles Marsh, *Strange Glory: A Life of Dietrich Bonhoeffer* (New York: Knopf, 2014), 176.

10 Geza Vermes, *The Real Jesus: Then and Now* (Minneapolis: Fortress, 2010), 178.

Chapter 5

1 Tom Stoppard, *The Hard Problem* (London: Faber & Faber, 2015), act 1, scene 2.

Chapter 6

1 Robert P. Jones, *White Too Long* (New York: Simon & Schuster, 2020), 185.
2 Martin Luther King Jr., *Where Do We Go from Here: Chaos or Community?* (Boston: Beacon, 1968), 38.
3 Bonhoeffer, *Letters*, 280.
4 Bonhoeffer, 281.
5 Dean Yeong, "The Fight of Two Wolves within You," deanyeong.com, December 17, 2017, https://tinyurl.com/24ckdn37.
6 *Methodist Worship Book* (Nashville: United Methodist, 1999).

Chapter 7

1 Rachel Held Evans, *Searching for Sunday: Loving, Leaving, and Finding the Church* (Nashville: Nelson, 2015), 208.

Chapter 8

1 Nadia Bolz-Weber, *Pastrix: The Cranky, Beautiful Faith of a Sinner and Saint* (Nashville: Jericho, 2013), 40.

Chapter 10

1 Richard Rohr, *Yes, And* (Cincinnati, OH: Franciscan Media, 2013), 40.

2 Mary Oliver, "Logos," in *Devotions: The Selected Poems of Mary Oliver* (New York: Penguin, 2017), 179.